A HISTORY OF

THE WORSHIPFUL COMPANY OF SCRIVENERS
OF LONDON

SCRIBITE SCIENTES

SCRIBITE SCIENTES

The Armorial Bearings of the
Master Wardens and Assistants of the Society of Writers of the City of London
incorporated by Letters Patent of King James I 28th January, 1617/18,
otherwise known as the Worshipful Company of Scriveners of the said City of London
which Arms were confirmed and Crest and Supporters granted by Letters Patent of
Sir Richard St. George, Clarenceux King of Arms, 11th November 1634

College of Arms
London

Windsor Herald and Registrar

A HISTORY OF

THE WORSHIPFUL COMPANY OF SCRIVENERS OF LONDON

VOLUME II

Brian Brooks & Cecil Humphery-Smith

Published for The Worshipful Company of Scriveners by

PHILLIMORE

2001

Published by
PHILLIMORE & CO. LTD.
Shopwyke Manor Barn, Chichester, West Sussex

ISBN 1 86077 119 X

Printed and bound in Great Britain by
BOOKCRAFT LTD.
Midsomer Norton

CONTENTS

LIST OF ILLUSTRATIONS

Frontispiece: The Arms of the Worshipful Company of Scriveners of London

PREFACE

BY

THE MASTER OF THE WORSHIPFUL COMPANY OF SCRIVENERS

It is fitting that the beginning of the new Millennium coincides with the publication of Volume II of the Company's history. Volume I, *A History of the Worshipful Company of Scriveners of London*, by Scrivener Francis Steer, was published in 1973 to mark the Company's sixth centenary. Dr. Steer's other major work on the Company is the *Scriveners' Company Common Paper 1357-1626*, which was published by The London Record Society in 1968.

This second book, Volume II, is the culmination of extensive research carried out by its joint authors, Past Master Brian Brooks (who worked with Dr Steer on Volume I) and the Company's Honorary Historian, Court Assistant Cecil Humphery-Smith. It is an important addition to the Company's history and also contains other valuable research material contributed by Past Master Oliver Kinsey, Honorary Court Assistant (and former Clerk) Peter Stevens, and Honorary Liveryman Stephen Freeth. Whilst being particularly concerned with the Company's recent history from where the first volume finishes (in 1880) until the present day, it also brings in the personalities involved in the earlier period.

The Company's history is remarkable. The second volume is a further important contribution to the history of the City of London, its social and economic change over the centuries, and the development of commerce, banking, and the law from the time of the Middle Ages. It deals with the many changes and challenges that the professional side of the Company has faced, and provides us with a further significant insight into the role of the Scrivener Notary over the last 700 years.

Today the Scriveners' Company embodies a strong core profession that maintains the highest standards of notarial practice as part of the City's role in the provision of professional services to international trade and commerce. Meantime, the civic side of the Livery Company plays an important part in supporting City government, and an equally essential charitable role in providing monetary aid that extends outside the City. The Company also continues to work to ensure that skills and craft disciplines, practised throughout its history, survive for the benefit of future generations.

This is a fascinating book for both reading and reference. I commend it to you.

NEIL GRIMSTON
Master (1999–2000)

ACKNOWLEDGEMENTS

In the course of our studies we have met with the kind assistance of many in record offices and libraries and with injections of useful and interesting material from several members of the Company past and present. We are grateful to them all. In particular we express our thanks to Sir Mervyn Medlycott Bt. for the research which he undertook, under Brian Brooks' supervision, into the 18th- and 19th-century biographies of members of the Company, to Peter Stevens for his erudite contribution to the historical information in Appendix IV regarding the Clerks of the Company, to Past Master and former Notarial Deputy, Martin Scannall, for contributing a description of the Scrivener Notary today in Appendix VIII, and to Andrew Hill (the Clerk of the Company), Irene Foan (the Assistant Clerk), Sir David Clayton Bt., Stephen Freeth, Melanie Barber, Irvine Gray, Philip Daniels, James Harman, Roy Lowlett, Alice Humphery-Smith, Peter Rumsden, Pat Mason, Lee Brace, Ann Mills, Michael Davies, Edgar Samuel, Ian Hilder, Gill Hunter, Christine Gregory, Judith Burns, and Angela Hannon for their help, and to the Immediate Past Master, Oliver Kinsey, for his contributions and for assisting in the editing of this work. We also express our thanks to Noel Osborne and his editorial team at Phillimore who have managed to put the many quarts of information into the pint pot of the present volume.

BRIAN BROOKS
CECIL HUMPHERY-SMITH
July 2000

Introduction

There may not be many Scriveners who are still engaged in engrossing documents in fine calligraphy with illuminated initials and borders, but, for the few who are, and for the Scrivener Notaries, there is still a livelihood to be made from scriveners' business, just as there has been for many centuries. The Scriveners' Company can be said to be one of the few City companies where there are still members who remain engaged in the trades and professions which gave rise to its foundation.

The abolition of the writing of Statutes of the Realm on to skins of vellum in a fine calligraphic hand, which has so destroyed the trade in tanning parchments and vellums, along with the replacement of the quill successively by patent dip pens, fountain pens, ballpoints, typewriting machines, word processing computers and the like, is perhaps to be regretted, but each year the Master of the Company presents to the Lord Mayor the quill pen which he uses on taking office at the Silent Ceremony in Guildhall. The Master also makes a similar presentation to the Sheriffs of the City, and to guests at Company dinners.

Francis Steer, the author of the companion volume to this history, was also a traditionalist. He had little interest in new-fangled subjects such as records' management. Computers would *not* have agreed with him. A stickler for administrative detail, in 1958 he was County Archivist of both West Sussex in Chichester, and of East Sussex in Lewes. Later he became Archivist of New College, Oxford, where there is a memorial to him in the cloisters. He was also a faithful servant of the Duke of Norfolk, working for many years as Archivist at Arundel Castle, and was appointed Maltravers Herald Extraordinary.

The project for Volume II of Dr. Steer's History was not completed at the time of the production of the first volume in 1973, but Steer also produced a remarkable edition of that marvellous medieval register, *Scriveners' Company Common Paper 1357-1628*, published by The London Record Society (Volume 4, 1968), which removed into the public domain most of the early documentation on the Company. Steer suggested examination of probate material and an extensive search has been made of the probate records of the Courts of London and the Home Counties. We have concentrated in this work on extracting biographical notes and looking to colour the history with the stuff of human relationships.

Listings and miscellaneous discoveries have been placed in appendices, as has a chapter covering the Company's adventures in Londonderry ('The Irish Estates') which would otherwise interrupt the narrative flow of this volume.

1
The Emergence of
The Scriveners' Company

The development of the guilds

Confraternities or guilds, often meeting in a common hall, date from the earliest times of commerce and craftsmanship. They were common in England in Danish and Anglo-Saxon times and continued to be established long after the Norman Conquest. The majority of these associations were religious in foundation. They were called guilds from the Saxon verb *gildan*, meaning to pay or contribute to a common purse. They provided a system of mutual undertakings between neighbours and kinsmen who joined together in order to preserve law and order, for self-protection and relief of poverty and suffering. Some of the guilds were also called frith guilds or peace clubs.[1]

In the towns, the frith guilds eventually amalgamated and developed into the trade and craft guilds and the merchant guilds. Their leader was called a warden and he and a quorum of guild brothers would form a court which enforced the ordinances agreed by its members. Unlawful tools or unworthy goods or products were confiscated and destroyed; disobedience was punished by fines, or, as a last resort, by expulsion. The latter involved the loss of right to trade. A common fund was raised by the contributions from the members. This not only made possible the objectives of the guilds, but enabled them to have masses said, to found chantries and to erect monuments in the churches where they worshipped in common, as well as to provide for communal dining on feast days.

The formation of trade guilds was encouraged by King Edward I, who found them to be a useful means of checking the lawless tendency of the barons. By the 13th century, wealthier citizens who found their old powers broken regained influence by enrolling themselves as members of the guilds, now called liveries because of the distinctive garbs and colours worn by the members of each craft. The labour laws of the reign of Edward III were introduced in order to control the malign influences of the guilds and the Statute of Labourers of 1389, in the reign of Richard II, was an appeal to craftsmen and workmen not to disturb the economy by fixing prices.

In 1436/7, a petition was presented to Henry VI by the House of Commons declaring that the craft guilds abused the privileges granted to them by enacting ordinances hurtful to the common profit of the people, and the powers and privileges of the guilds were then limited. The Acts of 15 Henry VI Chapter 6 (1436/7) and of 19 Henry VII Chapter 7 (1503/4) were designed to make guilds subject to the Chancellor, the Treasurer of England and the Chief Justices of King's Bench, Common Pleas, Exchequer or Chancery. The fellowships of craft, guilds and

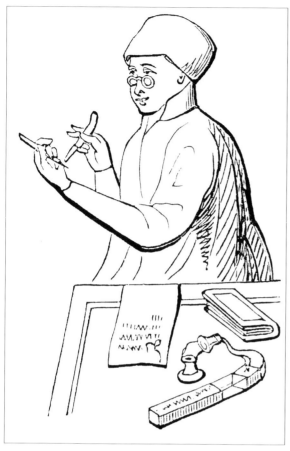

1 Portrait of a 15th-century writer from T. Wright, *Domestic Manners and Sentiments,* 1862.

fraternities were at this time found to be in many ways against the king's prerogative, the common law of England and the liberty of the subject, being (as Lord Bacon designated them) fraternities of evil.[2]

By degrees it would seem that a balance was struck between such excesses and the essential usefulness of these trade associations, and now, many centuries later, they have regained new life, and continue to have significant influence in the City of London.

As their name implies, the scriveners have always been writers. However, as Michael Birks wrote,

> The word 'scrivener' is apt to be misleading, for it might imply that he owed his origins entirely to his skill with the pen. This is not so; men did not employ him merely because his fingers were nimbler than their own, more accustomed to the feel of the sword or billhook. The scrivener earned his money, as much by his ability to compose documents, as by his penmanship.[3]

At the beginning of the 14th century it became common for members of the book trade to be named collectively as stationers, so-called because fixed stations were allocated to them where they could set up stalls and sell their wares. Those responsible for creating the medieval books were the parchminers who supplied the parchment, the scriveners who wrote the text, the lymners who created the illustrations and the bookbinders. It would seem however that, although participating in the production of the books, the scriveners themselves did not man the stations where the stalls were set up, since these, in addition to selling the books, sold pens, ink and all the oddments needed for writing. The scriveners would have set up their own stalls at fairs and in the market places and elsewhere, to which would come those who needed their services. Early in the Middle Ages, those who gave their services in markets, fairs and courts of law to writing letters and texts on lay, commercial and legal matters formed a fraternity or guild to enhance standards, to protect the integrity of their craft, and to provide charitable relief for those who fell upon hard times. They established the writing masters who taught subsequent generations not only the art of writing clearly, but also how to illuminate texts. The first official mention of a guild of Writers of the Court and Text Letter appears during the mayoralty of Henry Pykard in 1357. This also referred to the lymners and, curiously, the barbers.

When Adam de Bury was Mayor of London in 1364 general articles were promulgated for the proper government of all the crafts in the City. This was to ensure the integrity of all who were engaged in the crafts, thereby reflecting honour on those so engaged and giving confidence to the population at large which used their services. It was also decreed that four or six men from each craft should be chosen and sworn to see that this order was obeyed: penalties of imprisonment for 10 days and a 10 shilling fine were imposed on any member of a craft convicted of or rebelling against or hindering the order on the first occasion. Subsequent offences carried increased penalties as, for example, on the third conviction 30 days in prison and a fine of 30 shillings.

Like many fraternities, the scriveners took steps to protect their trade, particularly as a result of the influx of foreigners trading in money. Thus, there were considerable problems arising from the forgery of documents[4] as they became more important in the commercial transactions of medieval society. Only the royal personage was protected at law from the forgery of seals or letters, and, as late as 1371, Parliament rejected a bill to make forgery of private seals and the attachment to deeds punishable as a felony with imprisonment for life. Many of those who employed writers were illiterate and relied upon scriveners to be trustworthy in communicating the intent of their instruments, but clearly not all of them were as upright as they might have been.

The independent existence of The Scriveners' Company began with a petition presented to the Mayor and Aldermen on 26 September 1373 in order to obtain from the City the right to a separate craft. It recited that, as their craft was much in demand in the City, it was essential that those engaged in it should be lawfully and wisely governed. Reference was made to the fact that, for want of good rule, many mischiefs and defaults had been committed in the craft by those resorting to the City who had no knowledge of the customs, franchises and usages of the City, who called themselves scriveners and undertook to make wills, charters and other things touching the said craft, but the fact was that they were foreigners and unknown, and less skilled than the scriveners who were free of the City. The scriveners therefore asked their Lordships to grant firstly, that no-one should be suffered to keep shop of their craft in the City if he was not free of the City and made free of the craft by men of it, secondly that no-one should be admitted to the freedom if he was not first examined and found able by those of the same craft, thirdly that every scrivener of the City should put his name to the deeds which he makes so that it is known who has made them, and fourthly that everyone who should act against these Ordinances should pay 40 pence for the first time, half a mark for the second time and 10 shillings for the third time. The Mayor and Aldermen agreed that these rules should be henceforth observed and that the offenders should be punished according to these penalties. Unfortunately, however,

2   Book plate of Robert Wyer, flourished in 1527-47.

these Ordinances were not enforced, and the requirement that all deeds must bear the name of the writer was not observed, neither was the penalty inflicted. Not surprisingly this gave rise to further malpractices. One Thomas Panter, who set up in business as a scrivener although not qualified, was sent to the pillory. Such biographical material can be gleaned from the records of the City Remembrancer who was responsible for recording matters brought before the Court of the Lord Mayor for summary judgment.[5]

On 28 June 1391 the Bishop of London, Robert Braybrooke, issued a stern rebuke from his Manor of Stepney in particular against the practice of 'barbers and scriveners' for failing to observe Sundays and holy days. This led to further Ordinances being introduced in 1392, some of which (in particular the formal declaration to be given by freemen of the Company) survive to this day. In 1395 the Company's Wardens, Martin Seman and John Cossier, made a complaint to the Mayor that the Scrivener, Robert Huntyngdon, had for a long time been rebelling against them and disrupting the Scriveners' craft. The Mayor and Aldermen duly committed the mischievous Robert to prison until he conformed to his craft.[6]

In 1403 the 'reputable men of the craft of Writers of the Text Letter', the lymners and 'those wont to bind and sell books' petitioned the City for the right to elect a lymner and a text writer to be joint wardens of these trades. Thus started what is now The Stationers' Company. It was the company to which the Writers of the Text Letter, the lymners, the bookbinders and the booksellers belonged, and possibly the parchminers, too. Shortly after this the other branch of the scriveners (the Writers of the Text Letter) also parted from the lymners and each is shown in the City records to be a separate guild with its own Ordinances. The Scriveners' Company remained the Writers of the Court Letter and out of this role developed the notarial profession with which The Scriveners' Company has forever after remained closely involved.

The early history of the Company (which is described in more detail in Volume I) is largely accounted for in its efforts to establish control over the practice of all those writing legal documents in the City of London. These scriveners were engaged in making charters and deeds concerning land, making wills and sometimes acting as financial agents. From 1557/8, still a small Company in numbers but apparently increasing in wealth, the Scriveners, as well as members of other City livery companies, were compelled by the Crown to contribute to loans to recoup the costs of the war which resulted in England's loss of Calais. By 12 March 1589/90, with Elizabeth I on the throne, members were refusing to meet the Company's quota to pay for armour, weapons, gunpowder and wheat for Her Majesty's Service. The Master and Wardens of The Scriveners' Company were required to attend the Court of the Lord Mayor and Aldermen and were authorised to commit any member refusing to contribute to a debtors' prison.[7]

When a Royal Charter of Incorporation was secured from King James I on 28 January 1616/17 by the 'Master, Wardens and Assistants of the Society of Scriveners of London', a new era was opened. The Company's status was accordingly increased, though it is likely that its finances were considerably depleted. Indeed, it was the need to raise the money for the Common Council's Irish levy (described in Appendix VII) which caused the Master and the Wardens to petition the Lord Mayor and Aldermen for approval of their application to the King for their Charter. Under its authority, the Court of the Company was able to make new Ordinances and effect control over their craft. The Company was able to establish a monopoly over conveyancing within the City but was virtually ineffective elsewhere. The work of its members evolved into dealing as land agents and the confidential negotiations of loans and mortgages. Scrivening functions were insidiously eroded by attorneys whom the Company was unable to compel to become members, as can be seen in the chapter describing what became known as 'the case of the Free Scriveners' (p.22 *et seq*).

Although the Scriveners would seem to have been justified in introducing these Ordinances, the powers and monopolies of the craft fraternities were also resented, and it was felt that the abuse of these powers had caused much disservice to be done to the community. Some indication of popular conceptions of the behaviour of members of the craft during these centuries was captured in the verses of Thomas Hoccleve, entitled The Troubles of a Scrivener'.[8] Hoccleve described himself as a scrivener, and he was certainly a Writer of the Court Letter as a Clerk of the Privy Seal Office from 1387 at the age of 19 until his death in 1426. Geoffrey Chaucer, who died in 1400, also berated scriveners in *Troilus and Criseyde*,[9] and in 1577 Guevera wrote:

> As God made you a knight,
> if he had made you a scrivener,
> you would have been more handsome
> to colour Cordover skinnes,
> than to have written processes

In like terms is a later essay written in 1667 entitled *A Character of a London Scrivener*, reproduced in Appendix II, unkind as it is.

Notwithstanding these apparent shortcomings it was customary for the early guilds to bring the company of Heaven into their working lives, to thank the Creator for their skills and to invoke the saints to their aid. They established a calendar of religious occasions when they might meet together in prayer and later in feasting. This was done with great ceremony, which was also a means of inculcating respect and discipline into their young apprentices and generally keeping order. When the Scriveners' Company established Ordinances, the attachment to religious practice was strengthened.

Not unnaturally the Writers dedicated themselves to the Apostle and Evangelist, St John, as is reflected in their heraldry. St John the Evangelist is invariably symbolised in medieval iconography by the eagle which is often found to be holding a pencase and inkhorn in its beak. This provided the motif for the Coat of Arms used by the guild from at least 1530. Payment for accommodation in common hall, known as quarterage, was to be made on the Sunday after St John the Baptist Day. The choice of the Baptist rather than the Evangelist resulted from expediency, a June meeting being preferred to one in December.

After the Reformation, scriveners also became traders and brokers in money, bonds and bills, and dealers in imports and exports. Some scriveners practised the rudiments of banking in Queen Elizabeth I's reign, and Sir Robert Clayton, who started his career as an apprentice scrivener, went on to became one of the early directors of the Bank of England, and a leading political figure and philanthropist at the end of the 17th century. Sir Robert and other prominent scriveners who lived during the 17th century are described in the next chapter.

2

SCRIVENERS OF
THE EARLY CENTURIES

The first records of individual members of The Scriveners' Company owe their origins to a statute passed in 1388, pursuant to which every Sheriff of England was to receive two writs commanding him to make public proclamations throughout his shire.[1] The first called upon 'the masters and wardens of all the guilds and brotherhoods' to send up to the King's Council in Chancery returns of all details as to the foundation, statutes and properties of the guilds; the second called on the 'masters and wardens and overlookers of all the misteries and crafts' to send up in the same way copies of their Charters or Letters Patent where they had any. These writs were sent out on 13 November and returns were ordered to be sent in before 2 February in the following year. Interestingly, some of them marked their data 'forty years after the great pestilence'.

There were at this time no Masters of the Company. Wardens cared for all the affairs of the Company, perhaps with the assistance of the priest of St Anne's, the parish church nearest the Company's earliest hall, prior to the appointment of a Clerk. Martin Seman and John Cossier are referred to as Wardens of the Mystery of Writers of the Court Letter on 17 May 1392, having been elected as such on that day by the 'honest men of the craft of writers of the Court Letter'. They had been encouraged to do so by the Lord Mayor at that time, Adam Bamme, acting no doubt in accordance with the spirit of the statute of 1388. They and their successors are listed in Appendix III to this book.

The first Warden to be named as Master was John Dalton in 1583, and there follows an almost unbroken succession of Masters up to the present day as set out in Appendix III. However, somewhat confusingly, it was William Dodd who was named as the first Master of the Company in the Royal Charter issued on 28 January 1616/17 which gave the Society of Writers of the Court Letter of the City of London the jurisdiction encompassing the City and three miles therefrom which continued until 1999.

The first mention of the office of Clerk is in the same Royal Charter and Ordinances of 28 January 1616/17. John Plukenett or Plucknett, admitted on 9 December 1596, son of David Plukenett of Bridport, Dorset, yeoman, deceased, had been apprentice to Thomas Chapman. He was the first to be named as 'now Clerk to the Company on 6 July 1619'. Further details of the Clerks are set out in Appendix IV.

An attempt has also been made to build up a list of those who, following apprenticeship, by patrimony or under a master in the craft of writing to the Court

Letter, went on to become Scrivener Freemen. Subsequently they had the opportunity to engage in the governance of the Company through its Court, as wardens and masters. Later admission of non-practising scriveners by redemption adds some colour to the character of the Company's complement. Some freemen, of sufficient importance to deserve biographical notices, are collected together in Appendix V.

Particulars of scriveners have also been extracted from Deposition Books of the Prerogative Court of Canterbury, from 1658 (the earliest surviving volume) to 1665, and are reproduced in Appendix VI.[2] It is very evident that in the 17th century most people wishing to make a will (which they tended to delay until they were *in extremis*) would, rather than consulting a lawyer, send for the nearest scrivener, or call at his shop. In addition to writing the will, the scrivener was nearly always one of the witnesses to it and consequently was likely to be called as a witness or deponent in any legal dispute which might arise later and be dealt with in Doctors' Commons.

The *Common Paper* gives several examples of the forms of oath developed by scriveners in order to be seen to perform their craft with probity. These papers also record the names of many apprentices of the Middle Ages and the names of those who were their masters. Some distinction is made between masters in the craft and Masters who governed the Company after the Wardens appointed one of their number to be Master for the year. Similarly, there are distinctions made between apprentices and servants. Some records survive of the signs, symbols or marks used by individuals, especially notaries, to signify their work. There is also mention of those delinquents who avoided the religious services of the Company.

Almost all the Scriveners concerned were practising in London, though only a minority described themselves in court as 'Citizen and Scrivener'. Of the few outside London, the most distant were at St Albans, Basingstoke and New Sarum (Salisbury). Nonetheless, many of them had been born in remoter parts of the country. Luckily, the information asked of a witness, from 1662 but not apparently earlier or much later, included his birthplace as well as his age. The ages stated must be taken as approximate only, as may be judged from some of the statements made by deponents who appeared more than once, at different dates. There are interesting references to the Plague (1665) and Fire (1666) of London. In the printed indexes to P.C.C. Wills (up to 1700), occupations are indexed, and there are numerous Scriveners. As Dr Steer remarked in his *History*, '… these Wills would repay investigation, if it has not already been done'. Many have been examined and there are few references to the Scriveners' craft, while quite a number refer to creditors and debtors.

The first record of women being admitted to the Company was in 1665 when Elizabeth Billingsley was apprenticed to James Windus, who was Master in 1669, and his wife, Anne. Windus also presented Lucy Sanderson and Margaret Alsop as his apprentices in 1677, and Sarah Dutton was admitted to the Company by patrimony in 1675.

As will be seen from Appendix V, a number of Scriveners achieved prominence in the 17th century as Aldermen and Members of Parliament. Alderman Humphrey Shallcrosse (Master 1651) occupied the buildings adjoining the Company's Hall in Noble Street, as mentioned in the next chapter, and he was followed by four other Aldermen, namely Thomas Colwell (Master 1655), Martin Noell (Master 1659) who was a Member of Parliament and who was knighted in 1662, John Morris (Master 1670) and, perhaps the most prominent, Sir Robert Clayton (Master 1671) who subsequently became Lord Mayor of London, the first Scrivener to do so.

Robert Clayton was born in 1629, the son of a small farmer in Northamptonshire. He came to London to be apprenticed to his uncle, Robert Abbott, a prosperous Scrivener who was Renter Warden of the Company in 1658, and who, when he died, left Clayton a large sum of money. Clayton celebrated his 21st birthday in the year after King Charles I was beheaded, but it was another nine years before he married Martha, the 16-year-old daughter and heiress of a London merchant. Their marriage lasted for 46 years. Clayton was a contemporary of King Charles II, who returned to his throne in 1660. The restoration years provided the background against which Clayton set about building his career in the City and amassing a fortune which was to give him a commanding influence in the Councils of the City. In those days scriveners did not confine themselves to writing and conveyancing, but developed the business of bankers and estate management. In 1664 Clayton and his Scrivener colleague, John Morris, issued a cheque for £50 which is believed to be the earliest surviving British example of a banker's cheque.[3] Clayton and those who worked for him also managed extensive estates, including those of the 2nd Duke of Buckingham, and introduced the practice of double entry book-keeping to many landowners.

In 1671, at the age of 42, Clayton followed his colleague, Morris, who had also been apprenticed to Robert Abbott, as Master of The Scriveners' Company and introduced the concept of members of the Company being 'clothed' in the Livery and becoming Liverymen. In the same year he was elected Sheriff and knighted. Sir Robert was elected as a Member of Parliament and represented the City of London in seven Parliaments. He became Lord Mayor in 1679, the year of the Popish Plot, and he and Martha entertained the great and the good in their mansion in Old Jewry. The famous diarist, John Evelyn, described a private dinner he attended when 'the feast and entertainment might have become a king' and "his Lord Mayor's Show" was " London in lustre". He tells us that some envied Sir Robert's wealth, but without much cause, and he dubbed him 'Prince of Citizens'. Dryden described him as the 'Fantick Lord Mayor'.

Sir Robert was a notable philanthropist and he funded hospitals in particular. He was President of St Thomas' Hospital, and Vice-President of Christ's Hospital, where he built the girls' ward, and also of the London Workhouse. He became a director of the Bank of England in 1702, eight years after it received its Charter. He was a strong Protestant and a leading Whig, and his political fortunes followed those of his party. At the request of his constituents he moved for leave to introduce

3   Portrait of Sir Robert Clayton by John Riley, *c.*1670.

the famous Exclusion Bill to stop papists from succeeding to the throne. It passed through the House of Commons, but not the Lords. When the papist, James II, became King, he marked Sir Robert out for death, but Judge Jeffreys interceded to save him.[4]

With the country on the brink of another civil war Sir Robert was one of the deputation sent by the Common Council in 1688 to see William of Orange to persuade him to come and take the throne. After the Revolution he lent the new King £30,000, to pay off his Dutch troops. He died two years after his wife, in 1707, at the age of 78, and they are buried together in a vault in Bletchingley church in Surrey under magnificent monuments of white marble erected in their honour. Arthur Mee, in the Surrey volume of *The King's England*, describes his tomb as 'fashionable' and states that Sir Robert designed it himself. It is a fine example of baroque funeral architecture which shows Sir Robert wearing his robes and a gold chain, and Dame Martha, his wife, in a lace-trimmed dress and wearing gold earrings and bracelets. The plaque at the entrance to the vault describes Sir Robert as 'Scrivener - discounter of bills', and he was the epitome of the successful money scrivener. Sir Robert died childless and left his estate to his brother, William, who was created the first Baronet, from whom Sir David Clayton, the 12th Baronet, descends.[5]

3

THE HALL

(1628-1703)[1]

An early 15th-century deed refers to land identified as being near Beech Street as the site of the hall of The Scriveners' Company in the parish of St Anne (or St Agnes) in Aldersgate (now lost beneath the Barbican complex but once somewhere near the hall of The Butchers' Company). The hall was lost at an early date and the Company was making use of Wax Chandlers' Hall for dinners in the 16th century. There was an early association with the barbers of the City, possibly because, like the surgeons, who needed only the same tools as would cut a scrivener's quill, they were shop keepers in the sense of requiring little more than a table and chair for the performance of their craft. For some time, then, the Scriveners appear to have shared Barbers' Hall.

A tin trunk of miscellaneous papers and parchments from the 17th to the 20th centuries was delivered to the Guildhall Library in 1992.[2] The trunk contained the deeds, from 1631-1914, of the former Scriveners' Hall which stood on the east side of Noble Street and north side of Oat Lane. Since the realignment of London Wall after the war, the site is now immediately south of London Wall, and extends east from Noble Street up to the St Mary Staining garden, including the site of the present Pewterers' Hall. The Hall had been purchased by the Company on 10 June 1628 for £810 from Charles Bostock, citizen and scrivener, when it was described as 'that great house, formerly called Shelley House, and since called Bacon House, with a garden to the same belonging, in the parish of St Mary Staining, formerly in the occupation of Sir Nicholas Bacon, knight, Lord Keeper of the Great Seal of England (who rebuilt it in 1598) and adjoining the church and churchyard of St Mary Staining on the east, Oat Lane on the south, Little Silver Street (now Noble Street) on the west, and property formerly belonging to the late Abbot and Convent of St Peter's Westminster (Westminster Abbey) on the north'.

It would seem that the Company had bought one of the former aristocratic town houses of the City, and converted it to its own use. The building of Sir Thomas Shelley's house appears to have had the standard medieval pattern of a hollow square, with one side fronting the street, pierced with a gateway through to a central courtyard, and with some sort of great hall on the far side. It would have been something like Apothecaries' Hall, Master's Court at the Charterhouse, or one of the ancient Oxbridge colleges.

There are references in the deeds to 'improvements' made by the Company, i.e. to alterations rather than rebuilding. The cost of these may have caused the Company in 1642 to lease the range fronting Noble Street, including the space over the gateway, to Humphrey Shallcrosse, citizen and scrivener (mentioned above), for 99 years, for a downpayment of £200. By this date the whole building is referred to explicitly as Scriveners' Hall.

In 1649 the Company mortgaged the remainder of the Hall for £350 to Anne Yeend, a widow of Fenchurch Street. It is clear that the Company had by now leased this part of the Hall as well, this time to a John Reading, esquire. This suggests that the Hall may have already become a burden, and that it had to be rented out to make ends meet. The mortgage deed was witnessed, and probably written as well, by Christopher Favell, Clerk of the Company. Despite this, the Company was clearly intending to use the Hall for functions. The mortgage contained the stipulation that the Company was to have free access to the building for a minimum of eight and maximum of 12 days per year, 'for their meetings, keeping of Courts, dressing their dinners, and other their needful and necessary occasions and affairs'.

The mortgage was paid off in July 1658, and the Company then leased the Hall once again, for 31 years at £30 per annum, to William Parker of London, merchant. He again appears to have been in actual occupation. This time the Company's officers are described as having right of access to the

> halls, parlour, kitchens and room over the parlour … and free liberty to walk and be in the garden at such their meetings … and also free liberty for their great press, and their trunk with four locks and keys, to stand and be in the room now called the Music Room and for the said Master, Wardens and Assistants to lay up therein and take forth again at their pleasures such writings and other their goods remaining in and about the premises as they shall think convenient.

The trunk with four locks and keys would have been acquired by the Company to comply with clause 6 of the Company's Ordinances of 1619 which required three of the keys to be held by the Master and the Wardens and the fourth to be held by a Past Master or Warden. This must have been seen as a prudent precaution.

The deed of 1658 also contains a detailed schedule of fixtures and fittings in the Hall. This gives a picture of a gracious building with suitable ornament and pleasant garden on the eve of the Great Fire, which destroyed it completely. It included:

> two stone seats and an iron for a lantern before the street door; the Company's arms painted and gilded before the street door; the Courtyard and the two kitchens paved with hard Purbeck stone, a fair lead cistern in the courtyard, with two brass cocks and a wooden cover; and a pipe of lead to convey the river water from the street into the cistern ['river water' probably means the water supply from the New River Company, conduited from Islington; the water would appear to have been used for cooking, for drinking, and perhaps also for the garden, and for flowers in the courtyard] in the low hall, the room wainscotted round about six foot high, a wainscot settle bench on the north end and part of the west side, a court cupboard, a pair of racks and six halberds, three racks to lay pikes on, and a set of buck's horns in the parlour, the room wainscotted round up to the fretwork ceiling, a fair wainscot table, and two loose frames to set feet on, an iron fireback in the chimney and a

footpace (hearth surround) of black and white marble, and 18 red Russia leather back chairs in the great dining room, wainscot around 10 foot high, one fir table containing 26 foot in length painted all over having the City's and Company's arms set thereon, one little carving table, painted, one dozen red Russia leather chairs, a fair screen of wainscot wrought on both sides with three carved shields over the same painted and gilded with several arms thereon, an inscription in golden letters mentioning the enlarging and beautifying of the hall, and the Company's arms fair gilded in a large frame in the garden, two vines, two fig trees, and a stone roller with an iron frame to it.

All of this was swept away by the Great Fire in 1666. In 1674 the Master, Wardens and Assistants asked Thomas Raymond of Counsel whether they were empowered by their Letters Patent to levy a reasonable tax on members of the Company towards the costs of 'the re-edifying of the Hall'. By 1689 the Hall had been rebuilt, the 31-year lease of 1658 had expired, and the Hall was leased yet again, for seven years, to the Hudson's Bay Company at £60 per year. Once again, there is a detailed schedule of fixtures and fittings. It seems that no expense had been spared to replicate what had been destroyed. Plain staircases had been replaced with stairs with turned balusters, and there was some fancy furniture, including a folding Spanish sideboard with turned feet. Livery companies are very traditional, so there was also a new set of red Russia leather back chairs. There were also now three vines in the garden, as well as two fig trees as before, possibly the same ones, and, a new refinement, 'four large oaken posts for lines to dry clothes on'.

Unfortunately, the Company had probably overreached itself. In 1694 it had to mortgage the Hall, and the range fronting Noble Street, now consisting of four tenements, to John Riches of Christchurch, Surrey, esquire, for £400. By 1700 it had borrowed £200 more from him on the same security, making a debt of £600 in all.

By 1702 things were probably looking pretty grim, and the Company embarked upon a rearrangement of its assets. It sold some charity property on the Thames estuary at West Ham for £250. This was paid to Riches to reduce the debt. The West Ham property belonged to a charity set up in 1626 under the terms of the will of Nicholas Reeve, citizen and scrivener. The revenues of the property were to provide £10 per year to poor members of the Company.

The Court had realised that the West Ham estate produced less than £6 per year clear of the expenses of maintaining the sea wall at West Ham. It therefore now conveyed the four houses fronting Noble Street to trustees on behalf of Reeve's charity, and Riches accepted that only the Hall itself was still subject to mortgage.

Sadly, this was not enough. On 13 May 1703 the Company had to sell the Hall, except for the range now owed by Reeve's charity, to The Coachmakers' Company for a total of £1,600. Just under £500 of this went to pay off Riches, the mortgagee. The Coachmakers granted the Scriveners the right to use the Hall for five days a year for 51 years, which perhaps seemed a bargain since the Company had been entering into similar arrangements with its own tenants for many years.

The four tenements fronting Noble Street remained in the Scriveners' hands until 1914, when they were sold at auction, being described as 'warehouses, show-rooms and offices'. The Hall behind them continued as Coachmakers' Hall, and was rebuilt in the 1840s and again in the 1870s before being finally destroyed in 1940. Guildhall Library has a couple of sketches of the gateway and courtyard in the 19th century, but it is hard to tell the age of the structure depicted. The back part of the site, where the Hall proper and garden would have been, is now occupied by the post-1945 Pewterers' Hall.

4

THE EARLY EIGHTEENTH CENTURY: THE COMPANY IN DECLINE

In the early 18th century, after the forced sale of the Company's Hall in 1703, the fortunes of the Company declined. Some London historians were suggesting that the Company had disappeared from the City scene.[1] However this would appear to be erroneous bearing in mind the details that have survived of the Masters, and Clerks, as can be seen from Appendix III. These included the prominent Scrivener, John Ellis, who, as mentioned in the next chapter, testified in the Case of the Free Scriveners and described the work which he and his Scrivener colleagues undertook at that time. However, others, such as attorneys and notaries, practised conveyancing and became jurors of affidavits, particularly in foreign commerce, and the function of scriveners seems largely (but with some notable exceptions, such as Ellis) to have been transformed by the 18th century to an involvement in real estate and financial dealings.

The history of the Company between 1678 and 1732 is rather unclear because its records for those years have not survived. However some information about the Company has been obtained from other sources such as parish registers, wills and Chancery proceedings. Sir Robert Clayton has been previously referred to, since his life properly belongs to the earlier century, but for the purposes of this chapter it can be stated that he died on 16th July 1707 at the age of 77.

Samuel Dunklyn (junior), who became a freeman of the Company in 1722, and his father Samuel Dunklyn (senior), were defendants, with the brother of Samuel Dunklyn (senior), in proceedings brought against them in 1719 when a London merchant named Thomas Smith claimed that the Dunklyns had cheated him of his share in the partnership.[2]

Humphrey Brent, who practised as a Scrivener in the parish of Holy Trinity, Minories, acted for many years as the agent of Sir John Cass, a prominent City merchant who died in 1718 leaving a will which established the school in Hackney that bears his name.[3] By coincidence there has very recently been admitted to the Company Doreen Perry, chairman of governors of the Sir John Cass senior school, and the Company currently makes an annual donation to the School out of its Charity Fund.

Another prominent member of the Company who was involved in litigation in the Court of Chancery in this period was Mudd Fuller, a Scrivener by profession, who was Master in 1732-3. On 16 August 1726 he had purchased for £360 from the heirs of William Pursur some property in Ratcliff, just east of the City, which consisted of copyhold premises, 'with a wharf to the same belonging'.[4] The building

4   Print of Sir Robert Clayton's house, 8 Old Jewry.

had apparently been recently destroyed by fire so Mr. Fuller built a house on the site and moved into it. Two years later he borrowed £400 from Thomas Ryder, of Rolls Buildings, Fetter Lane, gentleman (perhaps an attorney) and his wife Carolina, having previously surrendered the property to the Lord of the Manor in favour of Thomas Ryder's wife before her marriage. In 1729 Fuller mortgaged other properties to a goldsmith and a cheesemonger. By 22 August 1729 he had 47 creditors, among them two members of The Scriveners' Company, Nathaniel

Gibbon and John Curryer. In order to obtain payment of these debts Fuller agreed to sell his property but was unable to do so. It seems unlikely that he recovered fully from these financial problems since his fine as an assistant was returned to him on 6 May 1742 and no will or letters of administration to his estate have so far been traced. It is clear from some other Chancery proceedings that Mudd Fuller had acted, in earlier years, as an investor for prosperous clients. In 1723 he was the holder of a power of attorney from Sir John Thornycroft 'for the disposal and placing out of a considerable sum of money'.[5]

In the Guildhall Library are the minutes of a Whig Club which existed during the last years of Queen Anne's reign and the early years of the reign of King George I.[6] The members of the club were City businessmen who supported the Whig party. Included in the minutes are lists of the names of individuals who were believed by the club's members to have political views which were considered dangerous by the government of the time. At a meeting of the members on 1 September 1715 a list was produced of 'suspected persons' in Broad Street Ward. One of these persons was John Taverner, a liveryman, and later a member of the Court of Assistants and Master (1717) of the Company, who had a scrivener's business in Threadneedle Street. The list, which included the names of several Roman Catholics who were living in lodgings in the City, was of importance because of the Jacobite Rebellion of that year.

The pollbooks for the City of London election in 1713[7] list all the City liverymen who voted, including 33 members of The Scriveners' Company. It is interesting to note that 18 Scriveners voted for the four Tory candidates, who were Sir John Cass, the City merchant previously mentioned, Sir Richard Hoare, the founder of Hoare's Bank, Sir George Newland and Sir William Withers. The four Whig candidates—Peter Godfrey, Robert Heysham, Thomas Scawen and John Ward—received 10 votes from members of the Company. Four members of The Scriveners' Company split their votes. The Whigs, who were the defeated party, threatened to query the outcome of the election, so two pollbooks were published separately by the rival candidates.

At the Guildhall Library there are lists of members of the Company from 1732 and also the wardens' accounts. The first list of members bears the heading 'Societat Scriptor Predict'. It gives the name of the Master, Mudd Fuller, and those of the Wardens, Philip Jennings and William Gwinnell. Mudd Fuller, as mentioned above, was a scrivener by occupation. Philip Jennings was a barrister and was M.P. for Queenborough 1715-22.[8] He was a grandson of another Philip Jennings who lived at Duddlestone Hall, Shropshire. His uncle, Admiral Sir John Jennings, was a Lord of the Admiralty. William Gwinnell was a cabinet maker and glass grinder whose premises, at the sign of The Looking Glass, were in St Paul's Churchyard.[9] Some indication of the extent of his business is provided by his trade card which states that he sold 'all sorts of Looking Glasses, Sconces, Coach Glasses and all sorts of Cabinet and Japan'd work; likewise all sorts of the Best and most Fashionable Chairs either matted or Carv'd, Blinds for Windows made and Curiously Painted on

5 *Hudibras and the Lawyer* by William Hogarth, 1700.

Canvas Silk or Wire.' He supplied the Common Room at St John's College, Cambridge with '20 Walnut chairs covered with leather at 14s. 6d.', these chairs being made to a pattern supplied by the College. Gwinnell's invoice for this work was submitted on 4 January 1736, 2s. 6d. being added to it for carriage of the pattern chairs. He was Master of the Company 1734-5 but became bankrupt in October 1741.

The list of the members of the Company compiled in 1732 gives the date when each member received his freedom and the method—servitude, redemption or patrimony—by which it was acquired. The Court of Assistants at that time consisted of 29 individuals. The other names on the list seem to be liverymen and freemen without distinction between these two categories of members. There are 109 of these names. It has been possible by research to establish the occupations of 20 of the members of the Court. Five of these individuals were scriveners by profession. There were four attorneys and four grocers. The other members con-sisted of a brewer, a dealer in wines and brandy, a paper hanging maker, a weaver, a jeweller, a merchant and a broker. The scriveners were John Taverner and John Curryer (who have already been mentioned in these pages) George Fox, Edward Dawgs, whose scrivener's business in Hatton Garden developed financial problems resulting in his bankruptcy in 1749,[10] and John Ellis, arguably the most prominent scrivener of the 18th century who is mentioned in the next chapter. Five of these members of the Court had been admitted to the Company by servitude to Henry Bedell, a scrivener and one of the Governors of the Charity School in Broad Street Ward who joined the Company in or before 1685 and died on 30 September 1728 when he was living and working in Threadneedle Street.[11] Two of the four attorneys mentioned as being members of the Court of Assistants were among these apprentices of Henry Bedell. They were John Knight, who became a freeman of the Company on 3 April 1693, and Nathaniel Gibbon, who received his freedom on 20 July 1726 and was Master 1735-6. The other two attorneys were William Stanlake, whose freedom was granted on 25 February 1690, and John Dwight, son of the Vicar of Fulham and grandson of the famous Fulham pottery manufacturer of the same name. He became a freeman of the Scriveners' Company on 3 February 1726. Stanlake, having served his apprenticeship to a member of the Company named William Waine, was admitted as an attorney of the Court of Common Pleas but did not take up his freedom of The Scriveners' Company, which brought an action against him in the Mayor's Court obliging him to do so.[12]

The members of the Company's Court in 1732 who had shops would no doubt have made their services available to other Scriveners. The Company accounts, for instance, contain a reference to a payment on 30 July 1751 to 'Mr James ffletcher for tobacco for the use of the Company'. He had a grocer's business in Knightsbridge at the time. Members of the Court may even have used the paper hanging services of their colleague Robert Dunbar whose business was in Aldermanbury. He certainly had clients of distinction since the accounts of the Duchy of Cornwall in 1738 show that he had supplied paper hangings for Cliveden in Berkshire where he installed '134 ps. white ground green popie Chince' for £26 16s. and '12 ps. of green on white borders' for £7 4s. Another of his clients was the Earl of Cardigan, who was married to Marlborough's grand-daughter. Dunbar supplied wallpaper for Lord and Lady Cardigan in 1740.

The list of freemen and liverymen in 1732 contains several entries for individuals against whose names the word 'mort' is written. One of the Scriveners who features in the list, and is mentioned in Appendices IV and V, is Jeremiah Bentham I, an attorney who was Master in 1725 and Clerk of the Company from 1731 until his death in 1741, when he was succeeded by his son, Jeremiah Bentham II, who is mentioned in the next chapter. Another attorney in the list is Josiah Bacon Lone who was apprenticed to Humphrey Brent, a Scrivener mentioned above, for a consideration of £60 on 31 July 1716. He duly served his apprenticeship of seven years, was admitted to the Company by servitude on 20 August 1723 and became Master in 1750. He died in 1753 leaving a will in which he asked to be buried in his own vault under the parish church of Christ Church, Spitalfields. One of his executors was his kinsman, Gyles Lone, a London notary.[13] It is clear from the list of members of The Scriveners' Company in 1732 that no notaries then belonged to the Company. In fact, it seems probable that notaries had ceased joining the Company about 100 years earlier or more. It is not possible to be more definite about this change in the Company's membership because no members' lists have survived between 1678 and 1732. An additional problem is that The Scriveners' Company Common Paper 1357-1628 with a continuation to 1678, which includes lists of members' details of apprenticeships and entries for notaries who belonged to the Company in the 16th century, contains no reference to any Scrivener described as a notary later than the reference in the entry to the apprenticeship in 1590 of Anthony Mason, a Yorkshire yeoman's son, to George Kevall, a London notary public who had become a freeman of the Company in 1559 and became Master in 1589.

5

THE CASE OF THE
FREE SCRIVENERS (1748-1760)

THE REPORT OF THE SCRIVENERS' COMMITTEE (1748) AND THE PETITION BY THE COMPANY TO THE LORD MAYOR (1749)

The encroachments of attornies and notaries, who were not members of the Company but who carried on conveyancing practices and the swearing of affidavits, particularly in foreign commerce, contributed to a decline in the Company's status in the early years of the 18th century. The Court of Assistants, concerned about the matter, appointed a Committee of its members to undertake a study of the position and to produce a report for consideration by the Master, Wardens and Assistants. This report was presented to the Court on 23 June 1748.

The Committee's brief was 'to take into Consideration and carry into Execution the Company's Charter, Constitution and Ordinances against Persons exercising the Art, Mystery or Occupation of Scriveners in the City of London and Elsewhere, within the Limits of the said Charter, who are neither free of the Company, nor of the City'.

The report began by stating that the Committee had examined the Company's constitution and the regulations by which it was governed showing that a scrivener's business was to make charters and deeds 'concerning Lands, Tenements and Inheritances, and all other Writings, which by the Common Law, or Custom of the Realm, were required to be sealed'. The report added that a scrivener's business could only be carried on by someone who was a freeman of the City and had been apprenticed to a London Scrivener for seven years.

The Committee had decided to make a full study of the constitution of the Company, tracing back its origins to the Company's petition in the reign of Edward III for Ordinances which would have the effect of enfranchising the Scriveners. This petition, delivered on 26 September 1373, has already been referred to, and was granted by the Mayor and Aldermen that same day.

Further Ordinances were granted from time to time, and were set out at great length in the Committee's report. These covered such matters as (in 1497) concern that some apprentices 'had not their perfect congruity of grammar' and the steps taken to rectify this.

Likewise there was the requirement that no one should be admitted to the freedom of the Company until he had been examined by the Master, Wardens and Assistants, or any six of them, on his competence to exercise the art of a scrivener and the ruling that no one could practise as a scrivener within the area defined by the Charter until he had become a freeman of the Company and sworn the oath of admission. The Committee's report refers, in addition, to the requirement that no one keeping a scrivener's shop should employ in it a person who was not free of the Company, that no scrivener should take an apprentice for less than seven years and that every apprenticeship should be enrolled in the Chamber of London.

Having studied the Ordinances and examined the Company's records, the Committee concluded that until 1665 the only individuals who practised the art of a scrivener were those who had been apprenticed for seven years according to the Custom of London. It was pointed out that in recent years attorneys and solicitors, although their work was very different from that of a scrivener, had taken on scriveners' work within the area covered by the Company's jurisdiction without the Company's inspection and regulation. The report also stated that many other individuals who had neither been apprenticed to the Company nor been admitted to it had set up as scriveners within the same area, and complained that, although the number of properly qualified scriveners had decreased in recent years, the actual business (some of it done by less qualified scriveners) had grown because of the great increase of trade in this country. This situation was due to the continual encroachment of attorneys and others, none of whom had the necessary qualifications. It was therefore, the Committee felt, for the good of the public in general that those who practised the art of a scrivener should be properly regulated and controlled. In those circumstances there 'would not be near so many fraudulent Deeds and Conveyances to give Occasion for Parties injured to apply to the Courts of Equity for Relief'.

The report argued further that the existence in the Company's records of the signatures of all its members would be of great assistance to aggrieved citizens who needed proof of the wrongs committed against them.

Another argument presented by the Committee's report was that, if all persons practising the art of a scrivener within the Company's jurisdiction were obliged to join The Scriveners' Company, the Company would be in the same position as other City Livery Companies such as the Surgeons, the Brewers, the Innholders, the Joiners and others which obliged non-freemen wishing to use their respective arts or trades to become free of the City and also of their respective Companies before being allowed to do so.

The Committee took Counsel's opinion on their conclusions and were able to report to the Company that Counsel agreed with them. They also expressed the opinion that it would be appropriate for attorneys and solicitors wishing to act as scriveners to join the Company, the expense of so doing being inconsiderable.

Having spent some time studying the origins and early history of the Company, considering the position in the City of attorneys and emphasising the importance to the public of scriveners joining the livery company of their trade, the Committee wrote in the final paragraphs of its report:

> This loss to the City of London of its Free Scriveners has been occasioned merely by
> neglecting to enforce the Custom of London against Non-Freemen using the Art of

Scriveners, in like manner as it is done almost every day against Foreigners occupying the Arts or Trades proper to other free Companies of the City.

By 'Foreigners' were meant individuals who were not freemen of the City. The Committee considered that this failure by the Company to exercise its powers was harmful to its interests and felt that if the Company was given by Act of Common Council powers similar to those possessed by other Livery Companies, such as the Innholders and the Joiners, to oblige individuals practising as scriveners to become free of The Scriveners' Company, a decision in their favour by the City authorities would not only increase the number of members of the Company but would also add to the number of Freemen of the City in general.

Finally, the Committee reported that it wished the Company to pray the Common Council,

> as the Protectors and Guardians of the Rights and Privileges as well of this great City in general as of every particular Company and the several Freemen thereof, to take note of the declining condition of the Scriveners' Company and to grant the Company an Act obliging all those who practised as scriveners in the area covered by the Company's jurisdiction to become freemen of the Company, to the Intent that they may become subject to the good Laws and Ordinances of it, and be brought under your Search, View and Regulation whereby all Frauds, Unskilfulness, Defaults and other Offences, in the Art, Mistery or Science of Scriveners, may more effectually be prevented or discovered and punished and that for the future no Person or Persons using or exercising the Art, Mistery or Science of Scriveners within this City or the Liberties thereof, may be made free of this City, by Servitude, Patrimony, or Redemption in any other Company than the Company of Scriveners.

The Court of Assistants gave prolonged consideration to this lengthy and well-argued report and decided to take the Committee's advice. They therefore presented a Petition in the spring of 1749 to the Lord Mayor, Aldermen and Commonalty of the City, asking for an Act 'to oblige all persons exercising the Art or Mystery of Scriveners within the City of London who are or shall be compellable to be free of the City to take up their freedom of the Scriveners' Company for its encouragement, to enforce the custom of London against foreigners exercising the said Art.'

The City replied to this Petition by informing the Company that 'the Scriveners' Company should first try their right to the benefit of the custom and By-Laws of the City in respect of persons exercising within the same the Art or Mystery of Scriveners', before the Committee made a report for granting the Act applied for on behalf of The Scriveners' Company, this decision being reported to the Company on 1 June 1749. The Court of Assistants then passed a resolution stating that the Company was bound in justice to its members to protect their rights and

> that a suit be forthwith commenced and prosecuted in the Lord Mayor's Court on behalf of the Company in the name of the Chamberlain of London against one of the Attorneys of the Courts at Westminster for exercising within the City the proper Art or Mystery of

the free Scriveners belonging to the Company by making and writing any deed or deeds, writing or writings, polled or indented, sealed or to be sealed, not being a freeman of London.

THE CASE OF THE CHAMBERLAIN OF LONDON V JOHN ALEXANDER (1749)

The Committee of Privileges, having been instructed by the Court of Assistants to deal with the matter, met on 8 June 1749 to consider the choice of a suitable attorney for the Company to sue.[1] The Committee resolved that 'twelve of the most eminent Attorneys-at-Law living within the City who are non-freemen, and exercising therein the proper art of the Company, should be named by ballot'. The attorney whose name was drawn first should be the one to be sued. The winner of this ballot was one John Alexander. A further resolution was then passed

> that Mr. Bentham, the Company's Clerk, do forthwith cause an action to be entered by the Lord Mayor's Court at the instance of the Company upon the City's Custom and By-Laws, against Mr. Alexander, whose name happened to be drawn first in manner aforesaid, for using within the City of London the art, trade, occupation, mistery, or handicraft of a Scrivener (the proper art of this Company), not being a freeman of the City of London.

The Company wisely decided, in addition, to retain Counsel in the Court of King's Bench 'by way of caution least the Defendant in such action shall by Writ of Privilege or otherwise try to supersede the said Action or control the Mayor's Court from proceeding therein.'[2]

Faced with these proceedings, John Alexander contacted his professional association, the Society of Gentlemen Practisers in the Courts of Law and Equity (precursor of the Law Society), to put it in the picture. At its Committee Meeting on 16 June, the Society agreed to defend the action in co-operation with him. Mr. Alexander then (as feared by the Company) issued a Writ of Privilege in the Court of King's Bench to restrain the proceedings in the Mayor's Court. The Scriveners took action to quash the Writ, but, on 10 November, the Court of King's Bench declared their opinion in favour of The Scriveners' Company and Lord Chief Justice Lee 'expressly recommended it to Mr. Alexander to submit and take up his freedom to qualify himself for exercising the said Art within the City'.

The Scriveners were naturally pleased with this result and instructed the Clerk to renew the petition for the Act before the Court of Common Council. They gave their Counsel a general retainer plus five guineas for each barrister and 10s. 6d. for each of their clerks.

The Company's accounts at this time include an item dated 29 January 1749/50 which reads 'Pd. Coachhire and expenses at The Golden Lyon, Temple Bar with Messrs Chauntrell, Ellis and Hussey, on attending the argument of the Company's affair against Mr. John Alexander in the Court of King's Bench 5s. 8d.' Edmund Chauntrell, a grocer, John Ellis, the prominent Scrivener mentioned above, and William Hussey, an attorney, were all Past Masters of the Company and members of the Company's Court of Assistants.

THE BY-LAW OF 1752 AND THE FURTHER PROCEEDINGS AGAINST MR ALEXANDER (1752–1756)

On 6 May 1752 after some delay, the Bill presented by The Scriveners' Company came up for discussion in the Court of Common Council and, after a debate lasting several hours, was finally passed, becoming the Act for Regulating the Company of Scriveners, London. It provided that from 24 June 1752

> every Person not being already free of this City occupying using or exercising or who shall occupy use or exercise the Trade Occupation Art Mystery or Science of Scriveners within the City of London or Liberties thereof shall take upon himself the Freedom and be made a Freeman of the said Company of Scriveners. And that no Person or Persons now using or exercising or who shall hereafter use occupy or exercise the said Trade Occupation Art Mystery or Science of Scriveners within the said City or Liberties thereof shall from and after the said 24th Day of June next be admitted by the Chamberlain of this City for the time being into the Freedom or Liberties of this City of or in any other Company than the said Company of Scriveners any Law Usage or custom of this City to the contrary notwithstanding.

The Scriveners' Company inserted in the *Daily Advertiser* and the *London Gazette*, at a cost of £1 5s., notices requiring 'persons exercising the art of Scriveners within the City of London to take up their freedom of this Company to qualify themselves for the same'.[3] As mentioned earlier in this account of the Company's history, there had been no notarial members of the Company for many years. However, it seems clear that the leading notaries in the City now decided that they must at least comply with the requirements of the Act. Therefore, on 29 May 1752, 10 London notaries became freemen of The Scriveners' Company by redemption. They were Benjamin Bonnet, of Threadneedle Street, Richard Parker, of George Yard, Lombard Street, Gyles Lone, of Birchin Lane, Thomas Brown and his partner Abraham Ogier, of Birchin Lane, William Tudman, of Birchin Lane, Charles Wiseman, of Castle Alley, Cornhill, Robert Shank, of Castle Alley, Cornhill, George Schutz, of Sweetings' Alley, Cornhill and Anthony Weldon, of Castle Alley, Cornhill. Four of these notaries later rose to the top of the Company, becoming Master: Bonnet in 1760, Ogier in 1762, Lone in 1770, and Shank in 1774.

In the meantime the Committee of the Society of Gentlemen Practisers had passed unanimously on 27 May 1752 a resolution that 'if any action should be brought against any Attorney or Solicitor on the general By-Law of the City of London, whereon the action against Mr. Alexander was founded, that such action should be defended at the expense of the Society.' Two days later a General Meeting of the Society passed resolutions agreeing with the Committee's decision and ordering that the text of the resolutions should be published in the *Daily Advertiser*, the *General Advertiser*, the *Gazetteer* and the *London Advertiser*.

On 4 June, two other notaries, Edward Faulkner and John da Costa, having taken out their freedoms of the Company the previous day, the Clerk reported to the Scriveners that, since the passing of the Act, several attorneys, to qualify themselves to practise as scriveners in the City, had joined other livery companies in order to become freemen of the City, contrary to the tenor and meaning of the Act. It was ordered by the Company that 'public notices be given in some or one of the daily papers that all persons who are not actually free of the City at or before the passing of the Act and who exercised the Art or Mystery of Scriveners after the 24th inst. would be liable to be sued by virtue of the Act in case they be not admitted into the freedom of the Scriveners' Co, notwithstanding such their freedom of any other Company.' This notice duly appeared in the *Daily Gazetteer* and on 10 June two attorneys, Adam Barber and Joseph Smith, joined the Company as did another notary, Solomon da Costa, and a scrivener, John Vaughan.

The Society of Gentlemen Practisers decided on 15 June to instruct an attorney named William Mason. On 24 June the Court of Assistants of The Scriveners' Company ordered 12 persons to take up the freedom of the Company in compliance with the Act of Common Council. Eight of these individuals, including Langley Hill who was Clerk of The Grocers' Company, were attorneys. Summonses were duly served. On 7 July the summonses served on four of the attorneys were read out at a meeting of the Select Committee of the Society of Gentlemen Practisers, which unanimously resolved to disregard them. However, the following day, Langley Hill approached the Company and asked to be given until the beginning of October to consider what decision he should take. In the meantime two more notaries, Samuel Willett and Moses Schomberg, and a scrivener, Robert Bowring, had joined the Company on 17 June. However, two attorneys, Thomas Wheatley and Daniel Highmore, tried to become freemen of two other livery companies, Wheatley selecting The Grocers' Company and Highmore The Wax Chandlers' Company. These attempts failed because the City Chamberlain announced that attorneys would only be granted the freedom of the City through The Scriveners' Company.

In the midst of all this activity the Chamberlain died, and so the whole matter was abated until a successor was appointed, whereupon proceedings re-commenced in the same manner as previously, several actions being entered against attorneys and others by the Chamberlain in support of the Company. Further postponement ensued because the Lord Chief Justice became ill and then died. Towards the end of the Easter term 1754 a new Lord Chief Justice was appointed, and so Mr. Bentham, the Scriveners' Clerk, went to see him, and handed him a copy of the Company's book. During the course of July 1754 disagreements took place between Bentham and William Mason, the Society's attorney, about the form of Court Order in the proceedings.

The Minutes of The Scriveners' Company at this time reveal that the Company, having discussed the rules, very sensibly ordered dinner. The meal began with:

> Five dishes of fish, consisting of salmon and trout, souls [*sic*], etc.
>
> Three dishes of Lobster, and shrimp sauce,
>
> Three hams,
>
> Four dishes of Chicken, three in a dish,
>
> Two venison pasties, and
>
> Four dishes of Colleyflowers, Cabbages, Carrots, etc.

These ample choices of first course were followed by

> Four haunches of venison,
> Four dishes of French beans,
> Four ducks in two dishes,
> Two currant tarts,
> Two raspberry and currant tarts, and
> Five stands of fruit

On 7 November 1754, the Rule of Court having been settled by the Judges, the case came on for hearing, but it was not until 16 November 1756, two years later and after further hearings, that the Recorder of London delivered Judgment against Mr. Alexander. Another year later litigation was still continuing until on 3 November 1758 the Judges confirmed the Recorder's Judgment. The Judgment was reported to the Court of Assistants of the Company which passed with satisfaction a resolution that 'the Master and Wardens should meet at the Rainbow Coffee House in Cornhill on the 8th and 15th instants to admit into the freedom of the Company all such Attornies-at-Law who should apply for the purpose'. It was decided that the following notice should be placed in the *Gentleman's Magazine*:

> 1758 (Friday 3 Nov.) Lord Chief Justice Parker, Mr Justice Dennison, Mr. Justice Clive and Mr. Baron Legg, four of the Judges who were appointed to give Judgment upon a writ of error in a cause depending between the Chamberlain of London, on behalf of the Scriveners' Company, and Mr. John Alexander, one of the Attorneys of the Court of King's Bench, for exercising the art or mystery of a Scrivener within the said City, not being free thereof, came to Guildhall to give Judgment, when they were unanimous in their opinion that the Judgment formerly given in the Mayor's Court, and which was in favour of the said Company of Scriveners, should be affirmed.

THE CASE OF HARRISON v SMITH (1760)

The Committee of the Society of Gentleman Practisers then decided that they would defend any further actions brought by The Scriveners' Company against individual attorneys and no attorneys applied to the Company for admission to the freedom. As the Company proceeded with additional actions against these attorneys matters began to move towards a trial in the Mayor's Court. In due course the trial took place at Guildhall on 11 December 1760 before the Recorder of London and a special jury of merchants who were not freemen of the City. The purpose of the action was to try whether John Smith, an attorney in the City of London who was not a freeman of the City, should be allowed to practise there as a scrivener.

Counsel for the plaintiff began by reading out the documents by which The Scriveners' Company was established and explaining to the jury that the members were 'people who have kept shops and were known to carry on their trade in shops'. The plaintiffs then produced three witnesses, all of whom were Scriveners. The first witness, John Ellis, a member of the Company, said that he had practised as a scrivener for 46 years and described the work which he and his colleagues undertook.

He was asked whether, during the course of his practice, he had known various scriveners who were 'very considerable' in the City. He replied in the affirmative and gave the names of several colleagues. All scriveners, he said, undertook conveyancing. Under cross-examination by Counsel for the defendant he said that scriveners acted as investment brokers in cases where they had been instructed to prepare the documentation. When Counsel said to him, 'You say there are a great number of opulent scriveners, but I fancy they did not all procure it by making deeds,' he replied, 'Yes, Sir, and they go to Newmarket and get a great deal of money there too.' Asked about attorneys in the City when he first started his business in 1714 he said there were very few attorneys who practised there then but most of them had taken out their freedom. As to Scriveners he said that 'Throgmorton Street was almost full of them'. The two other Scriveners called as witnesses provided information about their work which was similar to the details given by John Ellis.

Counsel for the defendant analysed the matters brought to the Court's attention by Counsel for the plaintiff and the witnesses. He ridiculed the contention that only scriveners could do conveyancing and said it was absurd to suggest that an attorney could not draw a Deed. In order to prove to the Court that attorneys had always done this category of work also he called as witnesses four attorneys who were then in practice. One of them said that although he had 'been an Attorney for forty years also doing Chamber business and conveyancing' he had never heard of a scrivener 'till within three years'. Another attorney, Mr. Hardin of Drapers' Hall, said that he had been concerned in the business of conveyancing for many years and had known many eminent attorneys who were not free of the City but had done conveyancing work 'and had not been interfered with by the Scriveners' Company'.

The defendant also called as witnesses three conveyancing Counsel who, in the course of their work, had dealt with attorneys, and one barrister who had previously been an attorney. This barrister, Mr. Webb, said that he had antiquarian interests and had searched through many ancient deeds in the Archives of the Dean and Chapter of Westminster, the British Museum and elsewhere, finding that only one in ten of such deeds was signed as a witness by a scrivener. The other two witnesses were an attorney, who was also a solicitor, and a solicitor who was not an attorney. They had both done conveyancing. Mr. Henshaw, the attorney who was a solicitor also, said that he 'considered it as a branch of the attorney's business to do conveyancing' and 'that he had never heard that it was an improper business for an attorney to be concerned in the City of London till it came into the City Cognizance.' He added 'really the reason given was a moving reason, but it did not move me. It was said that the Company was thrown into very great straits, and therefore must make use of this means to recover itself.' This statement was not wholly inaccurate for The Scriveners' Company had, indeed, been put to expense with all the litigation which it could not have afforded without the assistance of the Court of Common Council which had originally given it £200 towards its costs. It had, in fact, been obliged to make a second approach to this source of funding, from whom a further grant of £200 was received on 14 October 1760, just under two months before the case came on for trial.

The Recorder of London summed up by saying to the jury:

> You will consider that this is an action brought upon a By-Law which is calculated in order
> to secure the freedom of the City of London, and supported by a Custom of the City of
> London, which is formed into a By-Law for that purpose, and the words of the By-Law are
> 'that any person using the Art, Mystery or Occupation of a Scrivener within the City of
> London who is not free of the same incurs the penalty of five pounds'. The question is
> whether this is an Art and Mystery that falls within the By-Law. You will consider then the
> Evidence we have heard; what three witnesses have told you is the Art and Mystery of a
> Scrivener; they have told you that they look upon the making of deeds to be the Mystery
> of a Scrivener, now this is their description of it, and this is contraverted by the contrary
> party, they say it is the proper business of an Attorney to draw deeds. Now three Witnesses
> tell you that it is the proper business of a Scrivener to prepare deeds and arguments in order
> to be sealed, one says it is the business of an Attorney, and the other it is the business of
> a Scrivener. The Attornies admit they have done so, but they justify doing it because they
> are Attornies, now, Gentlemen, that is the question; you are to determine whether you think
> it the proper business of a Scrivener or an Attorney. If you are satisfied that it is the proper
> business of a Scrivener to draw these deeds then you are to give your verdict for the Plaintiff.
> If you are of opinion that it is the proper business of an Attorney then you are to give your
> Verdict for the Defendant.

The Court found for the Defendant. Eleven years of litigation had come to an
end.[4] Two of the Scriveners involved in the litigation were, however, particularly
noteworthy. They were the Company's main witness, John Ellis, and the Clerk,
Jeremiah Bentham, the son of the Jeremiah Bentham who was the previous Clerk,
mentioned above. Ellis, who can properly be called the doyen of the scriveners'
profession in the 18th century, was born in 1698. He was a money scrivener, who
lived and practised in Capel Court, and was probably the last of the practising
scriveners. He was Master of the Company in 1736, 1773, and 1784 (aged 86), and
he died in 1791, at which time he was still Deputy for the Alderman of Broad
Street Ward. As mentioned in his obituary which is quoted at the end of the next
chapter, he was also a writer of some distinction. He dined regularly with Samuel
Johnson (1709-84), the father of the English dictionary, and, as Boswell famously
recorded in his *Life of Samuel Johnson*,

> It is wonderful, sir, what is to be found in London. The most literary conversation that I
> ever enjoyed was at the table of Jack Ellis, a money-scrivener behind the Royal Exchange,
> with whom I at one period used to dine generally once a week.[5]

One can speculate that Ellis talked to Samuel Johnson about the litigation and
his long-serving Scrivener colleague, Jeremiah Bentham, who was Clerk of the
Company from 1741-92 and Master in 1777, and about Bentham's distinguished
son, Jeremy Bentham (1748-1832), the first of the utilitarian philosophers, who
expounded the principle of 'the greatest happiness of the greatest number' and may
not have grown up to have much sympathy for the cause which his father had lost
in the Case of the Free Scriveners.

6

THE LATE EIGHTEENTH CENTURY:
THE COMPANY POST-LITIGATION

The defeat of The Scriveners' Company in the Courts by an attorney supported by his professional association occurred at an important time in the history of this country—the accession to the throne of King George III on the sudden death of his grandfather on 25 October 1760, just over six weeks before the proceedings took place. The reign of the young King, who was 22 years of age when George II died, was to last for 60 years and to witness the occurrence of extraordinary events, such as the development of the spinning jenny by Hargreaves and the water frame by Crompton, the loss of the American colonies and the outbreak of the Revolution in France.

How did the Company react to these events and what was its situation, after protracted litigation, at the end of the 18th century? It is interesting to consider these questions.

The Company's Register of Apprentices, which has survived from 1756, gives details of all the individuals who were apprenticed to members of the Company from 16 March of that year. An examination of this register from that date until the end of the century shows that 126 apprentices were taken on by members of the Company during that period. When this figure is compared with the figures given in the Company's evidence during the litigation with the attorneys, it is clear that, following the court's decision against them, the Scriveners had reacted in a very positive manner by increasing their numbers.

Two of the apprentices taken during these years were women. They were Mary Harper who was apprenticed on 12 April 1758 to her mother Sarah Harper, widow of a grocer, and Christian Ramsay, apprenticed on 17 February 1763 to Mary Ramsay, a milliner.[1] Neither of these ladies joined the Company.

The Scrivener who took by far the largest number of apprentices during these years was Joseph Cooper (senior). Cooper was a successful carver and gilder in Noble Street where the Company had owned the Hall and still owned ground rents. He was Master of the Company in 1780. His apprentices numbered 26. Cooper's son, George Yardley Cooper, also a carver and gilder of 36 Piccadilly, had five apprentices during the period considered. William Davies, who had himself been apprenticed to Joseph Cooper, became free of the Company on completion of his apprenticeship, and set up in business, like his master, as a carver and gilder, and had six apprentices in those years. Another son of Joseph Cooper was Joseph Cooper (Junior) who was apprenticed to his father, became a freeman of the Company in 1779, a member of the Court of Assistants in 1795 and Master in 1801 and 1821.

The Company's lists of members in the second half of the 18th century have also yielded information about the individuals who belonged to the Company during those years. In 1750, the year after the Case of the Free Scriveners began, a draft membership roll was produced, to be followed by another such list in 1751. These lists give the addresses and occupations of many, but not all, of the members of the Company. Further lists were produced in 1758 and 1759. The list for 1760, the year in which the Scriveners' litigation with the attorneys finally ended, shows that the Master then was George Woodward Grove, an attorney, and the Wardens were the notary Benjamin Bonnet (mentioned above) and Adam Barber, one of the two attorneys who had joined the Company in 1752. The Court of Assistants consisted of 25 members. By 1774, when Richard Payne, an official at the Bank of England, was Master, and the notary Robert Shank (mentioned above) and Benjamin Vaughan (junior), a broker, were Wardens, there were 21 members of the Court of Assistants. They consisted of five attorneys (including the clerk), four notaries, two brokers, nine bankers, a merchant, a jeweller, a grocer, a bookseller, an apothecary, a perfumer, a hosier, a mercer and a scrivener (John Ellis, mentioned above). The list for 1799 shows that the Master in that year was a notary, Joshua Ogier, who was the son of Abraham Ogier, mentioned above, the Master in 1762. Of the 23 members of the Court of Assistants, five were notaries—John Mitchell, Tobias Atkinson, Thomas Bonnet, William Hammatt and Robert Robson. It is clear from the lists that since the end of the Company's litigation in 1760 many more notaries had acquired the freedom. The remaining members of the livery numbered 12, one of whom, Alexander Annesley, was both a notary and an attorney, practising in the City.[2] A number of additional notaries had, however, become freemen of the Company by 1799 but had not advanced to the status of liverymen.

Several of the notaries who joined The Scriveners' Company between 1752 and the end of the century had been born on the Continent or were descended from immigrants.[3] Richard Parker, for instance, one of the 10 notaries who became free of the Company on 29 May 1752, was born in Lisbon, son of an English merchant there. Benjamin Bonnet and Abraham Ogier, who were elected freemen on that day also, were of Huguenot descent; George Schutz was the son of a naturalised German. Two of the notaries, Samuel Willett and Moses Schomberg, who became freemen of the Company during those years were born in Germany, Willett's birthplace being Bremen and Schomberg's the Rhineland. Jacob de Pinna, who became a notary in 1772 and a Scrivener three years later, was born in Amsterdam, as were Soloman da Costa, Joseph Schabracq, Aaron Franco Drago and Peter Henry Hoogenbergh. John Rudolph Staub and Francis Gabriel Charles Müller were born in Switzerland. John Paul Dubourg came from Brittany. Claudius Holm was a Dane, born in Copenhagen. John da Costa was born in Spain. These men would, of course, have had linguistic ability which made them particularly suitable for notarial practice in London. Joseph Cortissos, for instance, who was a cousin of Jacob de Pinna and, like him, of Sephardi Jewish descent, stated on his notarial

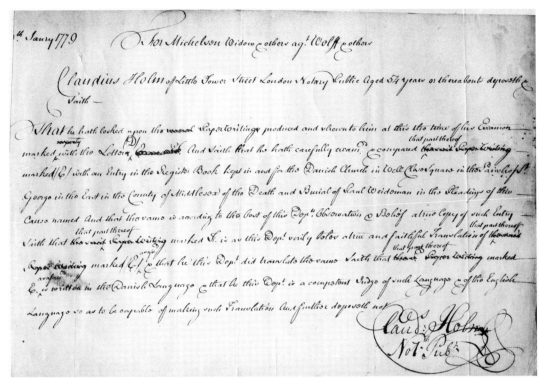

6 Affidavit by Claudius Holm, Notary Public, with reference to an entry in the parish register of the Danish Church in London.

faculty, which was issued to him on 6 July 1757, that his languages were Italian, Hebrew, Spanish and Portuguese. When he died in 1789 after a career during which he had built up a notarial practice based on these languages and had survived his bankruptcy which occurred in 1773, he left a will[4] reading as follows:

> This is the last will and testament of Joseph Cortissos of St Michael's Alley, Cornhill, Notary Public.
>
> As to my soul, I have always endeavoured to do harm to no one, to render justice to mankind, as far as in my power and, without hypocrisy, to praise my Creator, and to conform to His will, in all stations. In that consideration I find myself always prepared for death, trusting that whatever happiness there is in a future state, my soul will partake of it, through the infinite mercy of God, of whom I implore forgiveness for my sins.
>
> And with respect to my body, as I neither wish to grope underground, nor to be dissected after I am dead, especially as it has become a practice to steal the dead from the Jews' burial ground, it is my will and desire not to have my corpse buried until such time as putrefaction shall clearly appear, and that my corpse will not hold any longer. I desire that a high dry alcaly [sic] of pearl ashes dried on the fire be put in my coffin and spread over my body before I am buried, as an assistance to consume my flesh; that a sack of quick lime be put in my coffin and spread over my body before I am buried as an assistant [sic] to consume

the flesh, that a sack of quick-lime be laid under my coffin in my grave and another sack of quick lime poured on my corpse (which may easily be complied with by taking off the lid before my coffin is put in the ground); which done, that the coffin lid be laid on the lime and the earth over that; that then, the new-invented grave stone to prevent the stealing of the corpse, be sunk in my grave, where I hope my remains will be undisturbed.

And, with respect to my worldly resources, as what I leave is too trifling to direct a distribution of them, I give and bequeath all and singular of my estate and effects to my beloved wife Sarah Cortissos in which gift and bequest I comprise all my dictionaries, books, writings and precedents, and the whole register and records of my business, and recommend she give my papers, books and dictionaries to my sons Abraham and Josiah whenever they can make proper use of them if they take up my business, or to such of them as shall take up my business. Otherwise, to dispose of them as she shall think proper.

I give and bequeath unto my children, namely Esther, Sarah, Rachel, Abraham, Leah, Josiah and Hannah Cortissos, the sum of five guineas. Each of them to purchase a mourning ring or anything as a token and remembrance of a most tender father, whose only grief is that of not having been able to make a provision for them whilst living; trusting that their obedience to their mother, brotherly and sisterly love, uprightness to mankind, upright and honest deportment and fear of God, will supply that which I have not been able to do for them, and that industry will carry them through life, with decency and honour. I desire to have a common crape shroud, a plain deal coffin and four mourning coaches to my burial, and if more coaches are wanting, that they be hackney coaches; if my wife should choose to have a tombstone laid on my grave, let it be Portland stone with this inscription:

Here lays all that remains of Joseph Cortissos.

I desire my wife to provide decent mourning for herself and all my children, out of what effects I leave her. I direct her to pay my just debts, but that is, of course, as the Law directs. I desire my wife to apply to the wardens of the Synagogue to take back the grave I purchased of them at the side of my first wife, and that I may be buried in the line of graves in course at the time of my decease, and that my wife purchase a grave next to me. It being reasonable for her and my children that she and I lay next each other, I have no issue by my first wife.

I nominate and appoint my said wife, Sarah Cortissos, sole executrix of this my will, and, revoking all former wills and codicils by me heretofore made, declare and publish this, contained in the three foregoing pages, and this page, all of my handwriting, to be my true and last will and testament, to be good and valid, notwithstanding, what interlineations and obliteration of sentences or words shall be found therein, this being only the rough draft which I intend copying when opportunity offers and that I find leisure and time to do the same. In witness whereof I have signed these presents on this seventeenth day of June after Sabbath being my birthday when I enter my fifty-sixth year. I say this seventeenth day of June, one thousand seven hundred and eighty-six.

Joseph Cortissos.
1786.

I declare the contents to be the sentiments of my mind. 17th Novr 1788.

I give and bequeath to my dear and beloved wife all the rest, residue and remainder of my estate. I discharge my wife, from the trouble, from having the high dried alcolina being thrown into my coffin also of quick lime one at the bottom and the other on the top as I will not have any of that stuff.

Joseph Cortissos
We sign as witnesses at the testator's request and in his presence.

> Jos^h. Schabracq.
> Jb. de Pinna.
> 3rd Decr 1788.

Jacob Schabracq, one of the witnesses to Joseph Cortissos's will, was also Jewish as were several of the other notaries who entered the Company between 1752 and 1799. Schabracq was drowned in October 1799 when the frigate of war *La Lutine*, which was travelling from Yarmouth to Hamburg, was wrecked. In addition to the passengers, *La Lutine* carried £200,000 of bullion which was being sent to Hamburg to support the credit of the merchants of that city. When the bullion was recovered 60 years later it proved impossible to establish the identity of the underwriters to whom most of the money belonged so it was given to the Corporation of Lloyd's with the famous bell which they still own.[5]

Joseph Schabracq, like Joseph Cortissos, left a curious will,[6] made on 12 January 1788, in which he wrote:

> First, let me die where I will or fate should order it is my desire (if you please) to lay my dead body under ground. Second, I will and order that my present beloved wife and only friend I have in this world by maiden name Frances Ling, alias Fanny Schabracq, do enjoy possess and hold all and whatever I may leave behind at the time of my decease ... debarring every mother, sister, consanguinity or relation whatsoever or whosoever it may be from all, every or any claim demand or pretention whatsoever, hoping and desiring that if any one should pretend thereto the Law of this noble Land will protect my unhappy wife aforesaid, yet as I repose great confidence in my only worthy friends Messrs. Benjamin and Abraham Goldsmid, of London, merchants. ... [he appoints them his executors] ... desiring and begging them to have compassion of my poor unhappy, 'Though worthy, wife and as men of humanity and fortune not suffer my aforesaid worthy and good wife to become a victim to the same tempests I lingered my days away in and that 'though she is a Christian lay the blame on their deceased friend and pity her. Adieu, my ever dearest wife. Adieu executors. Do more than I can say. Adieu for ever, ever, ever. Adieu. Pray executors take care of my dearest wife. O pray do.

Attached to the will is a joint affidavit sworn by Michael Bedford, a friend of the deceased, and the deceased's mother-in-law, Ann Ling. Bedford swore that, as a most particular friend of Schabracq, he knew that he intended to leave his whole estate to his wife. Ann Ling deposed to the same effect. Michael Bedford continued the affidavit by stating that Schabracq had been asked by Messrs. Aaron Goldsmid,

Son & D. Eliason of London, merchants, on 4 October 1799 to undertake a voyage to Hamburg to execute business of great importance for their house. The deceased asked Bedford to superintend his business and family affairs during his absence and told him of the existence of his will and the provision made in it for his wife to receive the whole of his estate. When Bedford called on Schabracq again the next day, Schabracq said that he had brought the will from his counting house to his home in Lothbury and placed it with the lease of the house and other papers with Mrs. Schabracq. After the loss of *La Lutine* had been announced Michael Bedford went to Schabracq's house and, in the presence of Mrs. Schabracq and another lady, broke the seals on the will.

In the 18th century London notaries often acted as merchants and brokers in addition to their notarial work. Isaac Mendes Furtado, a notary who joined The Scriveners' Company in 1759, was also an annuity broker.[7] Robert Shank, in addition to his notarial practice, was in business as an insurance broker. His precedent book, which is extant, contains many references in 1753 and later to his connections with the shipping industry. Among the many precedent forms in the book, which include powers of attorney, bottomry bonds and charterparties, is an 'Assignment of a Negroe or Black', which reads as follows:

> To all to whom these presents shall come I Charles Eliot of London Mariner Send Greeting Whereas in and by certain Receipt or Bill of Sale bearing date at Suffolk in Nansimond County Virginia the 27 Sep[t] 1752 under the hand of Lemuel Riddick of said place Merch the said Lemuel Riddick Sold Transferred and Assigned to me the said Charles Eliot one Negroe Slave or Black Boy then named Jack Cut but now called by the name of Duke Now Know all men by these presents that I the said Charles Eliot for and in consideration of the Sum of £28.7. of lawfull money of Great Britain to me in hand at or before The Ensealing & delivery hereof by Sir John Ingilby of Ripley in the County of York at present in London Bar well & truly paid The Receipt Whereof I do hereby acknowledge myself to be therewith fully satisfied and thereof & of every part & parcell thereof do clearly & absolutely acquit Release & Discharge the said S[r] John Ingilby his Exors. & Administrators & Assigns & every of them for ever by these presents Have granted Bargained & Sold and by these presents do fully freely and absolutely grant Bargain Sell Assign Transferr & Sett over unto the said S[r] John Ingilby his Extors. Admors. & Assigns the said Negroe Slave or Black Boy now called Duke as aforesaid together with the said recited Receipt or Bill of Sale and shall my Right Title Interest property Profitt Claim & Demand whatsoever of in and to the same To have & to hold the said Negroe Slave or Black Boy unto the said Sir John Ingilby his Exors. Admors. & Assigns to his or their own proper use and uses & as his or their own property & Estate from henceforth & for evermore And I the said Charles Eliot for myself my Extors. & Admors. the said [the word 'Promise' is here crossed out] Negroe Slave or Black Boy unto the said Sir John Ingilby his Exectors. Admors & Assigns against all persons shall & will warrant & for ever defend & make good the aforesaid assign'd Negroe Slave or Black Boy against the Claims of any person or persons whatsoever free & clear of & from all manner of former and other Gifts Grants Forfeitures Claims or Demands by any way or means whatsoever In Witness Whereof I the said Charles Eliot have hereunto sett my hand and seal

the 19th day of September in the 27th year of the Reign etc. and in the year of Our Lord 1753 Sealed etc.

This document is followed in the precedent book by a form of receipt for the payment by Sir John Ingilby of the £28 7s. stipulated in the assignment.[8] This was a large sum which can be put into context by comparing it with the standard charges in 1797 for translations by notaries as laid down at a meeting of 15 members of the profession held at the *George and Vulture Tavern* in that year. For every folio of 90 words translated from Dutch, French or Flemish the cost was 1s. 6d. per folio and from English into those languages it was 2s. Italian, Spanish, Portuguese, German, Danish and Swedish translations into English were charged at 1s. 9d. and Latin at 2s. 6d. Notarial certificates as to the authenticity of translations cost 7s. 6d.[9]

Although the notaries who were members of the Company at this time are of interest, the careers of those members who followed other occupations have also repaid investigation. One of these members was Jonathan Warren, a blacking manufacturer, who joined the Company in 1768. He claimed to be the inventor of the original japan-blacking process and established premises at 30 Hungerford Stairs, Strand. Later he sold the business to a certain George Lamert who appointed as its manager his brother-in-law James Lamert. James Lamert, who was related to Charles Dickens and lived at one time with Dickens' parents, employed the author, then a child, in the dust and rat ridden warehouse which he had acquired. It was there that Dickens found himself working with a boy called Bob Fagin whose name he later used in *Oliver Twist*.[10]

The Company's records reveal, as indicated in the preceding paragraphs, that its reaction to the defeat which it suffered in 1760 was to encourage the London notaries to become members. That this membership was of importance to the notaries is shown by the entry for James Hennett, notary public, of 2 Essex Court, Middle Temple in the Law List for 1799, where he described himself, significantly, as a Member of The Scriveners' Company. Sadly, however, by this time the scriveners themselves no longer existed as a profession. When John Ellis, who had been a member of the Company for almost 70 years and (as mentioned above) had served three times as Master, died at the age of 93, on the last day of the year 1791, the *Scots Magazine* published an obituary of him, which read:

> He was, we believe, the last of that profession called Scriveners, which is one of the Companies of London; but the business now carried on by attornies and others. Mr. Ellis was a man of literature, and the pleasure he received from literary amusements remained with him till the last. He wrote some poems in Dodsley's Collection, and some hudibrastic translations; but never put his name to anything he published. He died suddenly in his chair, the lamp of life being totally exhausted. His faculties were entire and he was free from the mental imbecility and many of the bodily complaints, with which such extreme old age is attended.[11]

7

THE NINETEENTH CENTURY:
YEARS OF CONSOLIDATION

As mentioned in chapter 5, a number of London notaries joined the Company in 1752 to comply with the Scriveners' By-Law, and from then on they became increasingly prominent in its affairs, becoming dominant during the 19th century. In the years 1800-99 no less than 48 notaries served as Masters of the Company. Two notaries, the first John Venn and the second William Grain, served three terms. Six notaries served twice. The position of the London notaries in the 19th century was consolidated by the passing in 1801 of the Public Notaries Act which stipulated that, after 1 August of that year, no one was to be granted a notarial faculty who had not served an apprenticeship under articles for seven years to a notary or to a member of The Scriveners' Company who was also a notary. It also provided that all persons intending to practise as notaries within the area controlled by the Company should become freemen of it. Further Public Notaries Acts were passed in 1833 and 1843. In the first of these two Acts the Company's monopoly was extended to cover the City of London, the Liberties of Westminster, the Borough of Southwark and a circuit of 10 miles from the Royal Exchange. The Act of 1843 did not affect the position between notaries and The Scriveners' Company.

The 19th century also saw the emergence to greater prominence in the Company of various notarial families in the City of London. Although some of the London notaries during the 18th century had been related to one another, they did not all become members of the Company. Isaac Delpech, for example, who was notary to the Bank of England at the time of his death in 1736, and was the father of David Isaac Delpech,[1] a London notary whose widow married Benjamin Bonnet, also a notary and member of the Company as previously mentioned, never became a Scrivener.

The first London notary to establish a family which continued in notarial practice until recent times was William Newton, who received his faculty in 1775 but never joined the Company. At his offices in Cornhill he not only practised as a notary but also carried on business as a banker. His son, Benjamin Newton, qualified as a notary in 1789 giving his language as Italian, and joined the Company in 1808. He was also a member of The Joiners' Company. He served as Master of The Scriveners' Company in 1814-15 and 1826-7. The other members of his family who became London notaries were his son William Henry Newton who later emigrated to Australia, his brother John Newton (1785-1861), his nephews William Newton, John Newton (1816-90) and Thomas Edward Newton (1819-75), his

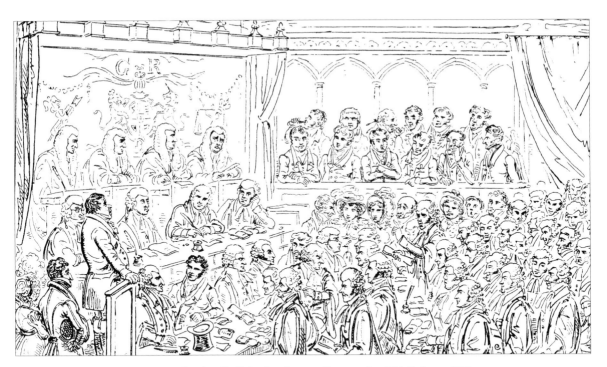

7 Engraving by Cruikshank of proceedings at the Old Bailey, c.1830.

great-nephew Douglas John Newton (1842-1902), his great-great-nephews Charles William Newton (1866-98) and John Edward Newton (1873-1949), his great-great-great-nephew John Newton (died 1979 aged 85) and his great-great-great-great-nephew John Newton. All these notaries named Newton became members of The Scriveners' Company except the second William Newton. John Newton, the sixth generation of the family to enter the notarial profession, died, sadly in early middle age, in 1964. He was the last member of the Newton family to enter the family firm, although his father, mentioned above, survived him until 1979. In 1865 the second John Newton had taken as his articled clerk and apprentice a stockbroker's son named Francis Jourdan who became a freeman of the Company by servitude on 9 November 1872 and a notary 10 days later, subsequently becoming Newton's partner. Jourdan's son-in-law, Henry Golding Freeman, joined the firm in due course. H.G. Freeman's son, Russell Jourdan Freeman, and his grandson, Patrick Francis Jourdan Freeman, who died in 1998, were all members of the Scriveners' Company and notaries in the City of London. Francis Jourdan, in addition to being a notary, ran a successful business as a foreign exchange broker. The writer was informed by the late Mr. R.J. Freeman that this particular firm of notaries—known latterly as John Newton & Sons—was established in 1761 by William Tudman. If William Tudman was the firm's founder, the date of its origins could be 1738 at the latest since that was the year when Tudman, one of the notaries who joined the Company in 1752, received his notarial faculty. The firm of John Newton & Sons continues in being to this day and is currently being run by Barrington Hooke, a freeman of the Company.

Another well-known notarial family was that of Venn, descended from Thomas Venn, who was a member of The Scriveners' Company but not a notary. The first of the nine members of this family who practised as notaries was John Venn (1778-1856) who obtained his faculty in 1800, having been apprenticed to the notary John Mitchell in 1793. He became a freeman of The Scriveners' Company by servitude in May 1800. The members of the Venn family who were notaries and members of the Company were John Venn's two sons John Sise Venn (1810-57) and William Webb Venn (1812-94), his grandsons John Venn (1839-1903) and William Webb Venn, junior (1838-96), his great-grandsons John Dalton Venn (1868-1952), Harry Peter Venn (1877-1943) and William Eustace Venn (1861-1922) and his great-great-grandson John Venn (1899-1985). All the notarial Venns served the Company as Master. John Mitchell, to whom the first John Venn was articled, became a freeman of the Company in 1773 by servitude to Robert Shank, previously mentioned in this narrative, whose notarial faculty was granted in 1751 and who joined The Scriveners' Company the following year. Robert Shank and John Mitchell practised in Sweetings Alley, Cornhill as notarial partners. John Mitchell subsequently took John Venn into partnership. Shank's partner as a notary had been George Schutz, mentioned earlier in this volume. Schutz obtained his faculty in 1729 so it could be said that the Venn family business was founded in that year or earlier. Known during the first John Venn's life as John Venn & Sons, the practice later separated into two firms, one run by the second John Venn and the other by his uncle the first William Webb Venn, to whom he had been articled. John Venn went into partnership with Horatio Arthur Erith de Pinna (1854-1912), who was the grandson of the notary Jacob de Pinna and the son of Abrão de Pinna (he was originally named Abraham but preferred the Portuguese spelling of his first name) who practised as a notary in the City from 1827, when he obtained his notarial faculty, until his death, at the age of 85, on 15 October 1879. His entry in the Law List for 1879 describes him as a 'Notary and Conveyancer only; Notary foreign and English to the Treasury and Notary Spanish and Portuguese to the Bank of England, Official Translator to the Admiralty and Probate Divisions of Her Majesty's High Court and to the Judicial Committee of the Privy Council'. His offices were at 71 Cornhill. He became a freeman of The Scriveners' Company on 14 February 1821 but never joined the livery. Horatio Arthur Erith de Pinna's son, Horatio Cortissos de Pinna, became a freeman of the Company and a notary in 1910. He was killed in action at Gallipoli, aged 27, on 24 October 1915 when he was serving as a private in the 1st City of London Yeomanry. He was the last notarial member of the de Pinna and Cortissos families.

In 1968 the firm of H. de Pinna & John Venn amalgamated with another old firm of notaries, Scorer & Harris, whose origins date back to the granting of a notarial faculty on 6 March 1765 to Tobias Atkinson, a yeoman's son from Westmorland who had come down to London as a young man. He became a freeman of The Scriveners' Company on 14 December 1774 and became Master 17 years later. He established himself initially at 3 Royal Exchange and 13 Angel Court, Throgmorton Street. As his practice increased he began to take in partners, beginning with another Northerner, Robert Robson, whose father was a farmer in Northumberland. By 1805 the firm had two more partners, John Withers and William Shackley. This was at a time when most lawyers were sole practitioners. Robert Robson died at Brighton, aged 52, in 1807 and was buried, appropriately for a notary appointed, like his colleagues, by the Archbishop of Canterbury, in the churchyard of St Mary's Church, close to the entrance to Lambeth Palace. His will shows that he owned property in Jamaica.[2] William Shackley having also died, Tobias Atkinson and John Withers took in as partner John Hayward Spenceley, who died in 1826. Atkinson died at Brighton in 1819 at the age of 75. There is a monument to him in Brighton's old parish church, St Nicholas. By 1828 the firm had three partners, John Tyndall Withers, William Scorer and Daniel Simon Merceron. William Scorer obtained his notarial faculty on 4 October 1816, giving his languages as Italian, Spanish and German. His articled clerk, Salem Constable Harris, qualified as a notary in 1843 and became Scorer's partner—hence the name of the firm Scorer & Harris. Harris's sons, Wilmer Matthews Harris (1852-1917) and Charles Berkley Harris (1858-90) later joined the firm. By 1908 the firm of Scorer & Harris had amalgamated with the firm of Grain & Sons, which had been established by William Grain, who became a notary in 1818. When two of his sons, William Grain, junior, and John Henry Grain, qualified as notaries they joined their father in partnership. The fourth member of the Grain family to be a member of The Scriveners' Company and a notary in the City of London was the late Felix William Grain, a great-grandson of the first William Grain. He was a partner in H. de Pinna & John Venn for many years and ran the firm's West End office at 41 Whitehall.

The firm of Cheeswrights derives from William Dunbar, a Scotsman who obtained his notarial faculty on 30 November 1771 and became a freeman of The Scriveners' Company on 13 January 1780. He was admitted to the Middle Temple on 21 November 1775 and called to the Bar on 24 November 1780.[2] He was thus both a notary and a barrister. In his will,[3] which is dated 6 December 1798, he described himself as 'of Nicholas Lane, London, Notary Public and also for the eighteen years last past an honorary barrister-at-Law of the Honorable the Society of the Middle Temple, London'. A sentence in his will reads, 'I do not pretend to dictate but I cannot help suggesting that one of my sons should follow the business of a Notary (along with such other addition as may be found expedient).' Neither of his sons followed his advice but Dunbar's notarial practice continued after his death as he had taken into partnership another Scotsman William Duff, who had been articled to him. William Duff joined The Scriveners' Company on 17 June 1801 and was Master 1807-8. His brother Archibald Duff, an attorney, also joined the Company. He was Master 1810-11. William Duff's sons, William Duff junior and John Rutherford Duff, also became notaries and members of the Company, as did

John Rutherford Duff's sons, George Daniel Duff and Brookes Duff. John Rutherford Duff fell on hard times and became bankrupt in 1840, at which time he had
become a wharfinger. In 1851 he was employed as an accountant by a railway
company. His brother, the second William Duff, prospered and survived the other
notarial members of his family, dying, aged 85, on 29 December 1882 at his house
in Bayswater. Before his death he had taken into partnership John Bridges and
Charles Joseph Watts, both of whom had been articled to him. Bridges and Watts
both had sons who became notaries and members of The Scriveners' Company.
Their firm was Duff, Watts & Co.

The first member of the Cheeswright family to qualify as a notary and become
a freeman of the Scriveners' Company was Henry Cornfoot Cheeswright, whose
notarial faculty was issued on 31 August 1838 after completion of his articles to his
uncle Lewis Gilson, junior, whose notarial practice had been started by Thomas
Clark in 1779 and who practised as a notary for many years at 62 Lower Thames
Street. Lewis Gilson, junior, was also a shipbroker and Custom House agent in
partnership with his father Lewis Gilson, senior, who was admitted as a notary on
10 January 1789, becoming a freeman of The Scriveners' Company on 29 July
1795. Both the two Gilsons and Henry Cornfoot Cheeswright were freemen also
of another City Company, the Fishmongers'. Cheeswright and the younger Gilson
worked in partnership offering their firm's services from the premises in Lower
Thames Street as well as from Milford Haven in Pembrokeshire[5] until Gilson's
death on 3 December 1844 at the age of 46. In 1851 Cheeswright engaged his
nephew Frederick Cheeswright as an articled clerk and apprentice. They became
partners after Frederick Cheeswright had qualified as a notary. The notarial business
had been extended to the ownership and insurance of vessels.[6] Henry Cornfoot
Cheeswright died at the age of 73 on 6 June 1889. Frederick Cheeswright then
practised on his own until his son Stanley Cheeswright qualified as a notary on
9 December 1896, having joined The Scriveners' Company in July. Unfortunately,
Frederick Cheeswright died, aged 58, on 15 November 1897, less than a year after
the granting of his son's notarial faculty and serving as Renter Warden. As a result
Stanley Cheeswright had to continue the business as a sole practitioner as his father
had done. Fortunately, however, he had taken an articled clerk and apprentice,
Lindsay Ralfs Casey, shortly before his father's death. Casey qualified in 1905 and
became Cheeswright's partner. When Stanley Cheeswright died in 1921, the
connection of the Gilson and Cheeswright families with the notarial profession
came to an end. However, about 10 years later the firm of Cheeswright & Casey
merged with Duff, Watts & Co. The present firm of Cheeswrights represents both
these old notarial practices.

The notarial firm of Comerford & Co, which merged with H. de Pinna and
John Venn in 1940, was started by James Comerford who obtained his faculty as a
notary on 5 April 1796 but did not become a freeman of the Scriveners' Company
until 27 July 1825. His son, James Comerford, junior, obtained his notarial faculty
on 15 December 1827, having joined The Scriveners' Company the previous month.

His father was at that time in practice at 27 Change Alley, Royal Exchange, with a notary named Thomas Samuel Girdler.[7] The younger Comerford joined the partnership which adopted the name Comerford, Son & Girdler. James Comerford, senior, died on 11 August 1833. The second James Comerford was a scholarly man who became a Fellow of the Society of Antiquaries and had a well-known library. He lived for many years in St Andrew's Place, Regent's Park and had a country house at Framfield in Sussex, where he was buried after his death in London on 8 March 1881.[8] The Comerford family possessed in 1963 a miniature of him painted about 1831 by François Rochard, the well-known portrait painter.[9] James Comerford's son, a notary and member of the Scriveners' Company like his father before him, was named James William Comerford. He was twice Master of the Company (in 1868-9 and 1901-2). He also served as a Deputy Lieutenant for the County of London. After his death in 1916 two of his sons, Alan Charles Comerford and Robert Homfray James Comerford, both members of The Scriveners' Company, continued his notarial practice. The late John Martyn Dimond, a notary who qualified in 1923 after serving articles with Comerford & Co, used to tell amusing stories of the antediluvian way the firm was run during his days there. One of the partners used to spend a great deal of time a) changing his mind about what holiday destination he should select and b) washing his hands, which presumably acted as a receptacle for all the dust that accumulated in the office. The telephone system, he said, had become so antiquated that eventually there was only one engineer in London who knew how to repair it when it broke down. It was no tremendous surprise, therefore, for the partners of H. de Pinna & John Venn when Comerford & Co amalgamated with their firm, to find that the list of clients was short, consisting almost exclusively of the Westminster Bank. The connection of the Girdler family with the notarial profession was continued by Thomas Samuel Girdler, junior (1850-1923), son of the first James Comerford's partner, and Joseph Girdler Walker, who was Thomas Samuel Girdler senior's stepson. Joseph Girdler Walker's son Edwin Courtney Walker, notary and Scrivener, became a partner in Scorer & Harris. Edwin Bruce Walker, the son of Edwin Courtney Walker, who died in 1961 aged 96, also practised in the City as a notary, but is now retired.

There were five other families which contributed four or more notarial members to The Scriveners' Company. They were the families of Gibson, Nichols, Armistead, Donnison and Burwash. The Gibson and Nichols families, which were related to one another, included no fewer than 12 London notaries, the first of whom was William Gibson, whose notarial faculty was issued on 28 January 1758. He practised for some years in Bow Lane[10] but never joined the Company. His son, William Gibson, junior, also a notary, became a freeman of the Company on 18 January 1775. He and his father practised in partnership initially in Bow Lane and later at 9 Lombard Street for many years.[11] The second William Gibson died in 1807 and was buried in the Church of St Mary Woolnoth.[12] Two of his sons, William Henry Gibson and John Holmes Gibson, joined the family notarial business. William Henry Gibson became a notary in 1792 but does not seem to have taken

up his freedom of The Scriveners' Company. John Holmes Gibson, who joined
The Scriveners' Company on 10 April 1811, was both an attorney and a notary.
He was also a Common Councilman in the City for Langborn Ward 1817-27
and 1845-51. He practised for some years at 79 Lombard Street in partnership with
his two nephews William Nichols, who served as a Common Councilman for
Langborn Ward 1828-32, and George Gibson Nichols.[13] John Holmes Gibson
eventually retired, leaving the firm to be run by the two nephews who were later
joined by William Nichols's son James Worthington Nichols. Gibson died at his
home in Ramsgate in 1865 at the age of 91. His grave there[14] is marked by a
monument on which his daughter Caroline, who had died at Boulogne, aged 20,
many years earlier, is also commemorated. Her commemoration takes the form of
a poetic tribute which, as an example of its kind, is perhaps worth recording:

> There was a snowdrop on the bed,
> Green taper leaves among,
> White in the driven snow its head
> On the slim stalk was hung.
> The wintry wind came sweeping out,
> A bitter tempest blew,
> The snowdrop faded never more
> To glitter with the dew.
> Then let us think on death,
> Though we are young and gay,
> For God who gave us life and breath,
> Can take them soon away.

This verse was to prove relevant to the fates of the remaining notaries of the
Gibson and Nichols families. The two nephews only survived their uncle by two
and three years respectively. William Nichols died in 1867 and his brother George
Gibson Nichols the following year. James Worthington Nichols died, aged 29, in
the same year as his father. His brothers, William Martin Nichols, George Livesey
Nichols and Alfred Ernest Nichols, all died in middle age. William Martin Nichols
became insane and died in the Surrey County Lunatic Asylum, Wandsworth in
1887 at the age of 54. George Livesey Nichols had to apply to the Scriveners'
Company for assistance in 1885 as he was unemployed and in 'distressed circumstances'. The Company granted him 10 shillings per week for a year. This allow-
ance seems to have been continued for another 12 months but when Mr. Nichols
applied for further assistance on 9 November 1887 this particular application was
refused and instead he was offered a payment of £20 per annum 'if his sons wished
to emigrate'. This curious condition was declined. Poor Mr. Nichols lived on for
another four years, finally expiring at his home in Leytonstone at the age of 48 on
15 May 1891. One of his sons was working in that year as a valet in Piccadilly.
Alfred Ernest Nichols, the youngest of these three notarial brothers, was found dead
in bed at his home in Upper Norwood in 1884. The coroner's certificate gave the

cause of death as apoplexy. The deceased notary was only 39 years old. Although the Nichols branch of the family ran the notarial practice, towards the end of its existence two other relations named Gibson had also qualified as notaries and been associated with it. They were John Gibson, the son of John Holmes Gibson, who became a freeman of The Scriveners' Company and a notary in 1825, and John Gibson's son, William Gibson, who obtained a faculty in 1853 but never became a member of The Scriveners' Company.

The Armistead family were Quakers. Five members of this family, four of them notaries, were members of The Scriveners' Company. William Armistead, a Yorkshireman, came down to London and became a notary in 1790. As a Quaker he made an affirmation for the Faculty Office instead of an affidavit. He became a freeman of The Scriveners' Company on 29 July 1795, having previously joined the Worshipful Company of Wheelwrights. He entered into notarial practice in Clement's Lane with another Quaker, Edmund Barker Allen, who was also a freeman of the Company. When William Armistead died in 1825 at the age of 70 he left his house in Clement's Lane and the residue of his estate to his son Thomas Gumersall Armistead, who was also a notary. To another notarial son William Armistead, junior, he left £5 'hoping his conscience will convince him of the justice of my bequeathing him so small a sum after his slanderous and wicked conduct towards me'. William was to receive a further £10 on condition that he gave no trouble to the executors, one of whom was his brother. To another son, Francis Armistead, who ran a business as a coal-merchant and wharfinger at Heston and was a freeman of both the Stationers' and the Scriveners' Companies, he also left £5 'considering his conduct on several occasions extremely reprehensible and undutiful'. Francis, he said, owed him £1,570 which was to be paid in full with interest to the executors. If this was done the amount of the debt would be reduced to £340.[15] William Armistead, junior, lived and practised as a notary until he died on 30 January 1844. His brother Thomas Gumersall Armistead followed him to the grave 11 months later. The fourth notary in the Armistead family was Alfred Armistead, son of William Armistead, junior. He died unmarried in 1881.

John Donnison, who became a freeman of The Scriveners' Company on 13 May 1812 by servitude and Master in 1844, was a master mariner's son from South Shields. He was articled and apprenticed at the age of about 13 to Thomas Ferguson, a London notary who was also a member of The Scriveners' Company. His articles were subsequently transferred to Ferguson's nephew, Abraham Peell, also a notary and member of the Company. Having obtained his notarial faculty in 1812, Donnison set up practice at 63 Fenchurch Street where he specialised in shipping work. In 1825 he was Secretary to the Thames Association for the Mutual Insurance of Ships. Later he took into partnership his sons John Donnison, junior, and James Donnison, the firm being named John Donnison & Sons. He died in 1858 and both the sons died unmarried within a week of one another three years later. Another of John Donnison's sons, Alfred Donnison, was only 22 years of age and was still under articles to his brother John when this brother died on 23 January 1861. His articles were then assigned to William Duff, with whom he remained nine months. At the end of that time his articles were further assigned to John Venn. On completion of his articles he obtained his freedom of The Scriveners' Company on 3 December 1863 and his notarial faculty five days later. Although there must have been an interregnum in this firm's business between the deaths of the two brothers in 1861 and Alfred Donnison's admission as a notary in 1863 the office, which had been at 71 Cornhill for at least twenty-four years, remained there. Alfred Donnison's son John Alfred Donnison, who qualified as a notary and joined The Scriveners' Company in 1890, becoming Master in 1904, became a partner with his father in the notarial firm. Alfred Donnison died in 1912. When John Alfred Donnison died in 1936 his firm became part of the notarial practice of Scorer & Harris.

Another notarial family was that of Burwash. David Burwash, son of a clockmaker in Clerkenwell, was articled on 20 March 1829 to Arend Jacob Guitard, a Dutchman who obtained his notarial faculty in 1798 and practised as a notary for many years at 26 Birchin Lane but never joined The Scriveners' Company, although his son Charles Frederick Guitard, also a London notary, was a member of the Company and served on the Court of Assistants. Burwash became a freeman of the Company and qualified as a notary in 1836. Three of his sons, Frederick David Burwash, Edwin Augustus Burwash and Sydney Burwash, all became notaries and members of the Company, joining their father in his notarial practice. The four notarial members of this family all died within a few years of one another. Edwin Augustus Burwash's death occurred on 24 February 1875 and that of his father on 11 September 1876. Sydney Burwash and Frederick David Burwash both died in 1879. Sydney Burwash's death took place on 24 February of that year, four years to the day after the demise of his brother, Edwin Augustus.

In addition to the members of notarial families who joined The Scriveners' Company there was another family of London lawyers which produced several Scriveners. This was the family of Nelson. The first member of this family to become a freeman of the Company was George Nelson, a London solicitor who obtained his freedom by servitude on 9 November 1790, having been apprenticed to another solicitor, William Wheatley Hussey, who was the Scriveners' Clerk. He practised for many years in Essex Street, Strand and eventually succeeded Hussey as Clerk of the Company in 1805, holding that position until his death in 1828. He was in turn succeeded as Clerk by his nephew Park Nelson, who remained in that position until 1876. He was also a solicitor. The firm of Park Nelson, solicitors, is still in existence. George Nelson's brother, John William Nelson, joined the Company in 1809 and was Master 1818-9. Park Nelson married his first cousin Catherine Anna Maria Nelson whose brother, George Nelson, junior, also a solicitor, became a freeman of the Company in 1823. The fifth member of the Nelson family to join the Company was Robert Rogers Nelson, a solicitor, who married in 1866 Mary Chauncey Maples, daughter of Frederick Maples of the well-known firm of City solicitors Young, Maples, Teesdale & Nelson, in which he had become a partner.

The other branch of the legal profession which was represented in The Scriveners' Company was that of the proctors, who were the equivalent in the ecclesiastical courts of solicitors and attorneys. They practised in Doctors' Commons. Two proctors joined the Company during the 19th century. They were Philip Charles Moore and Frederick Clarkson. Moore, who became a freeman on 20 May 1829, married in 1828 Margaret Rosa Darlot, daughter of Henry Darlot, a notary who practised for many years in the City but never joined the Company, having obtained his notarial faculty the year before the passing of the Public Notaries Act in 1801. He died at Hastings in 1849, aged 43. Clarkson joined The Scriveners' Company in 1843 and was Master 1852-3. He died in 1861. Doctors' Commons was abolished by the Judicature Act of 1875, the work of the proctors being undertaken thereafter by solicitors.

Reference has already been made in these pages to certain foreigners who joined The Scriveners' Company during the second half of the 18th century. This process continued in the 19th century. Christopher Sundius, for example, who became a freeman of the Company on 4 April 1810, was a London notary born in Sweden in 1754, the son of a Lutheran pastor. After completing his studies at Lund University he entered the Swedish Naval Cadet School and a year later began active service in the Swedish Navy as an extra cadet on board a frigate. In 1774 he passed his examinations to become a Lieutenant. In 1777 King Gustavus III of Sweden agreed to send five of his naval officers for service in the Royal Navy.[16] France declared war on Great Britain in 1778 and the following year Sundius took part in an attack on Fort Ravell in the island of Hispaniola. In 1780 Sundius and the other five Swedish officers were ordered to leave the British navy and enter the French service. Sundius applied for and obtained a discharge from the navy of his native country and became a volunteer in the Royal Navy. On the conclusion of hostilities by the Treaty of Paris in 1783 Sundius resigned from the navy and went into business in the City. While serving in the British navy he had become an ardent Methodist and had married an English lady named Ann Richardson. At the time of their meeting she was planning to sail for India but, according to the History of the City Road Chapel, 'as she loved God with her whole heart, she preferred uniting herself to Mr. Sundius and enjoying the privileges of religion among the Methodists to the brighter worldly prospects offered to her in India'. During the 14 years of their marriage the couple had 10 children, six of whom survived infancy.

Sundius established himself in the City of London initially as a ship and insurance broker. He obtained a notarial faculty on 18 February 1793 but did not obtain his freedom of The Scriveners' Company until 4 April 1810, perhaps because he was already a freeman of another City Company, the Farriers', which he had joined in 1791. He became a member of the Scriveners' Court of Assistants just over a year after entering the Company. By 1805 he was trading as a Russia merchant at 58 Fenchurch Street with a partner named Alexander Shirreff and practising as a notary and translator in Fen Court, Fenchurch Street with a fellow notary, Frederick

Pfeiffer.[17] He had also become a Director of the London Missionary Society,[18] a member of the committee of the Preachers' Friend Society and a Trustee of the City Road Chapel. In addition he had joined with others in 1804 to establish the British and Foreign Bible Society. Generous by nature, he made extensive gifts in 1808 to help Swedes who had suffered in the war against Russia and also took part in the campaign to alleviate the misery caused in Germany by the Napoleonic Wars. His wife having died, he married in 1798 Jane Vazeille Smith, who was the step-grand-daughter of John Wesley and had often accompanied Wesley on his preaching visits to various parts of the country. Sundius and his second wife had eight children, five of whom survived their infancy. Unfortunately, as the Napoleonic Wars were coming to an end, Christopher Sundius found himself in financial difficulties and on 17 June 1815, the day after Wellington's victory at Quatre Bras, he became bankrupt. However, his notarial partner, Frederick Pfeiffer, remained loyal to him and the business continued to exist, another notary, Stephen Noad, having joined the firm by 1818. By 1 November 1828 Sundius and Pfeiffer decided to dissolve the partnership because of Sundius's deteriorating health. Noad had set up on his own several years earlier. Christopher Sundius died, aged 80, on 2 March 1835 and was buried in the family grave at the City Road Chapel. He left a will which provided for his immediate family and included numerous bequests to charities and Swedish relations. In it he thanked his wife for all her kindness to him during his 'protracted feeble state of health' and gave his blessing to her, his children, his grandchildren and his daughter-in-law, ending this lengthy document, executed on 19 May 1830, on a fine patriotic note with the words 'God save and bless King George the IVth and old England'.[19]

During the first half of the 19th century two other London notaries who were born on the Continent became members of The Scriveners' Company. They were Barnard van Sandau and Isaac Philip Blanquet. Van Sandau, born at Homburg in the 'Domains of His Prussian Majesty', as his notarial faculty put it, became a notary in 1789, but did not obtain his freedom of the Company until 13 April 1813. He practised for many years at 7 Pope's Head Alley, behind the Royal Exchange, and died in 1849 at the age of 89. Isaac Philip Blanquet was born at Dieppe and articled to George Guillonneau, a London notary whose family were originally French, on 28 March 1811. He was granted a notarial faculty on 29 May 1820, having joined the Scriveners' Company three days earlier. Guillonneau took him into partnership at his office at 2 Pope's Head Alley, Royal Exchange. The partnership was dissolved in 1838. No reference to Blanquet's death can be traced in England or Wales up to the end of 1850 so perhaps he returned to France. During his years in London he translated from French a work by one Charles le Brun with the impressive title *A Series of Lithographic Drawings Illustrative of the Relation between the Human Physiognomy and that of the Brute Creation … with Remarks*. The book was published in 1827. Guillonneau retired from practice and died, aged 67 and unmarried, at his home Causey Ware Hall, Lower Edmonton. He left no will so letters of administration were taken out by his sister and only next of kin. His estate amounted to £120,000.

References have been made in this narrative to members of the Company who were Quakers and Jews. In the early 19th century two Irish Roman Catholics became freemen. On 27 July 1801 Thomas McKiernan, who came from Waterford, qualified as a notary, receiving his authorisation to practise from the Archbishop of Canterbury's Faculty Office. He swore a special form of notarial oath and became a freeman of The Scriveners' Company on 27 June 1805. He became a freeman of the City of London on 11 July 1805. Two years after Thomas McKiernan's admission to the Company another Irish Roman Catholic, Hugh Bourke, obtained his freedom and swore a similar notarial oath. He practised as a notary for some years in Gracechurch Street. The oaths which both these notaries swore on their admission are interesting as they omitted the anti-Papal references contained in the oaths normally sworn at that time by notaries, attorneys and solicitors.

As already stated in these pages, one of the most distinguished members of The Scriveners' Company was Sir Robert Clayton who was Lord Mayor of London in 1679. Over a century was to elapse before the Company produced another Lord Mayor, but this did occur in 1805, when James Shaw, who had joined the Company in 1798, was elected to that office. He was a Scotsman, born at Riccarton, near Kilmarnock, in Ayrshire in 1764. He established himself as a merchant in the City, becoming also a Director of the West India Docks and the Imperial Insurance Company. As Lord Mayor he entertained the Prince of Wales 'attended by his royal brothers and a long train of nobility, at a civic feast in the Mansion House'. At Nelson's funeral, during which many members of the Royal Family took part in the procession, he exercised the City's right to precedence on public occasions. During the period of his service as Lord Mayor he was also Upper Warden of the Scriveners' Company so he became Master in the year 1806-7. He was also a Conservative Member of Parliament for the City 1806-17 and City Chamberlain from 1831 until his death. He was created a baronet in 1809.[20] After his death, which occurred at his home in the City, 11 America Square, on 22 October 1843 at the age of 79, the *Gentleman's Magazine* published his obituary which is of considerable interest and reads:

Sir James Shaw, Bart. Oct. 22

At his house in America Square, in his 80th year, Sir James Shaw, Bart, late Chamberlain of the city of London, President of the Royal Artillery Company [*sic*], and of the London Lying-in Hospital, a Director of the West India Docks, and of the Imperial Insurance Company, and a Visitor of the London Institution.

He was born at Riccarton, in the county of Ayr, Aug. 26, 1764. His family, though highly respectable and honourable, were in circumstances too confined to allow scope for the enterprising spirit of their numerous offspring, and James with his brothers quitted at an early period their paternal home, to seek advancement under more favourable auspices. James, by diligence, integrity, and ability, graduated from the lowest seat in the counting-house of an eminent mercantile firm in the city to the distinguished position of a partner in the house. In 1798 he was elected by the inhabitants of Portsoken, the ward in which he lived, to the

8   Portrait of Sir James Shaw by Mary Martha Pearson.

office of Alderman. He became Sheriff of London and Middlesex in 1803, and in the year 1805 he was elected Lord Mayor.

On the day previous to his quitting the civic chair he was elected, at the general election, one of the members for the city, which position he occupied in three successive parliaments, until the dissolution of 1818, when he retired. In Sept. 1809 his Majesty was pleased to confer upon Mr. Shaw the dignity of a Baronet; and in Jan. 1813 he received a second patent, with remainder to his nephew John Shaw, of Whitehall Place, esq. the son of his sister Mrs. Margaret Macfie, and who had previously taken the name of Shaw by royal sign manual in 1807. Sir James Shaw had a grant of arms allusive to his civic honours, with figures personating Fortitude and the City of London as supporter. In the hand of the former was placed a scroll, inscribed 'The King's warrant of Precedence' alluding to the firmness with which, during his mayoralty, he asserted the privileges of his office.

Sir James, during the whole of his parliamentary career, was the warm supporter of the Conservative administration which then wielded the destinies of the nation; but though a constant, he was an independent supporter of the party, and never was known to have asked for or received either place or emolument for any of his numerous family and connections, for whom he otherwise had to make provision. Sir James continued to discharge the duties of Alderman with scrupulous impartiality and unvarying punctuality, until the year 1831, when, upon the decease of Mr. Richard Clarke, he was elected to the lucrative and honourable office of Chamberlain of London, which he continued to hold until he resigned in May last.

It may be recollected that Sir J. Shaw had invested 40,000*l.* held by him as the banker of the corporation in spurious Exchequer-bills, with which a year or two ago the money-market in the City was inundated. A considerable portion of the emoluments of his office was derived from the temporary employment as a banker of the surplus cash and securities in his hands not required for immediate use. This had often been considered an objectionable mode of paying a public servant; but still, as the particular mode of investment was left to the discretion of the officer, he was responsible for the validity of the instruments on which he made the advance. The writer of this brief sketch was called upon to advise his friend a few hours after the astounding intelligence of the invalidity of these bills had reached his ear. He spoke upon every part of the subject in a tone of calm and dignified resignation. He produced from his pocket a small scrap of paper, on which, with his usual neatness, were figured down the particulars of his property in India and Bank Stock, or Dock shares, and other available securities, against which he had placed the value at the price of the day, and, with a fervour that came from the bottom of his heart, thanked God, although it would scarcely leave him 500*l* it sufficed to meet this unexpected calamity, without giving to the corporation or his sureties the slightest occasion for anxiety or alarm. While this matter was under the consideration of government, great fluctuations in public opinion took place as to the probable result. Knowing that upon the event depended the only provision made, as well for his declining years as to sustain the honours of the title, a friend communicated to Sir James that speculators were willing to take the chances of the result, upon being allowed a moderate discount for the risk and delay; the face of the venerable man for a moment wore an unusual flush; 'No', was his reply, 'were I to take 17s. 6d. in the pound, it would betray a doubt of the propriety of my demand, or a doubt of my country's justice. I shall patiently abide the issue, and will not sacrifice an iota of my claim'. Though he appeared to bear the trial with great equanimity, there is no doubt that it tended to hasten the event to which his malady was preparing the way. It was the subject of great satisfaction to him to be able personally to attend the commissioners to whom the inquiry in the Exchequer-bill fraud had been intrusted, and before his resignation as Chamberlain he had the additional consolation of receiving the whole amount of the bills with interest to the day of payment.

Sir James Shaw was at all times a pattern for the performance of his official duties, punctual to all his appointments, and precise in all his arrangements. As Chamberlain, it was his duty to hear all complaints of masters against their apprentices, and apprentices against their masters. Such was the effect of his firm but conciliating tone, that it has been frequently known to subdue the most resolute and obdurate spirit, where mildness without firmness, and vigour without judgment, had been tried in vain. His office has witnessed many scenes of the deepest interest. Masters and apprentices, parents and children, whose deep-seated anger it appeared impossible to appease, have been melted by the influence of kindness, and have had to bless the day their disputes were heard before one who knew how to temper justice with mercy, and to administer law with judgment and discretion.

Perhaps there are few men who have contributed to the advancement of so many deserving young persons as it was his good fortune to promote. The walls of his drawing and dining rooms were crowded with the portraits of many of those objects of his patronising care. To the corporation school he gave annually 100*l*. To a vast number of the charitable institutions, which constitute the glory of the nation, he was a generous contributor. To well-founded applications to his bounty a five or a ten-pound check was always ready, and the last day will alone reveal the numberless recipients of his private charity.

Two days before his decease, his medical attendant deemed it right to intimate to him that his sojourn on earth was near his close. He received the communication with the composure with which a good man meets his fate. After sitting up in his bed for a short time on Sunday evening, he sunk back on his pillow, and without a sigh or a groan expired. 'Mark the perfect man and behold the upright, for the end of that man is peace.

Sir James's will[21] included bequests to various charities including Sir John Cass's School. He bequeathed his portrait to the Corporation of London and expressed a wish to be buried in Sir John Cass's vault in Aldgate Church. If this was not possible, he wished to be buried in the Church of St Lawrence Jewry. His baronetcy became extinct in 1868.

Another baronet who was a freeman of The Scriveners' Company was Sir George Gerard de Hochepied Larpent, whose baronetcy was conferred on him in 1841. He was a merchant and East India agent in the City and was M.P. for Nottingham 1841-2. He became a freeman and liveryman of the Company on 11 February 1847. He died in 1855. His baronetcy became extinct in 1899.

Although the membership of The Scriveners' Company has usually consisted of individuals who earned their livings in the City, it is interesting to note that one of the Company's most distinguished members in the 19th century was a theatrical and musical agent and manager named John Mitchell who owned a book shop in Old Bond Street. He joined The Scriveners' Company in 1849 and served on the Court of Assistants before becoming Master in 1857. His shop was well known and had many eminent customers, including Queen Victoria and the Emperor Napoleon III. John Mitchell was also very prominent in the musical world of early Victorian England. In 1837 he introduced opera buffa at the Lyceum Theatre, staging for the first time in this country many operas including Donizetti's *Betly*, which had received its première the previous year at the Teatro Nuovo in Naples, and Rossini's *L'Italiana in Algeri*, which had appeared many years earlier and is still frequently performed. Subsequently and for many years he put on comic operas and plays at the St James's Theatre, engaging famous actors of the time such as Rachel. In 1842 he introduced Rossini's *Stabat Mater* to London audiences. 'Few men', says *Grove's Dictionary of Music and Musicians*, 'were better known in musical circles. Whatever he did was done as well as he could possibly do it, and he was esteemed and beloved as an honourable man of business and generous friend.' He died on 11 December 1874 at his London house in Bolton Street. In his will he bequeathed to his son two gold snuff boxes, one presented to him by King Louis Philippe and the other by Napoleon III, and also a claret jug given to him by the Duke of Brunswick. Another gold snuff box, given to him by Sir Henry Bishop, composer of 'Home Sweet Home', he left to his friend, the Victorian composer, Sir Julius Benedict, who wrote in his diary on 12 December, 'my poor dear old friend Mitchell died yesterday, 10 o'clock p.m. of bronchitis. I lost more than a brother in him. He can never be replaced but lives for ever in my memory'. Other bequests in the will included a clock, formerly the property of Field Marshal the Duke of Wellington, which had been presented to him by Wellington's son. Mitchell's son, George John Mitchell, who was associated with him in the bookselling business, was also a freeman and liveryman of The Scriveners' Company, which he joined in 1874, the year in which his father died. He was in the brewery trade, his father having bought him a partnership in a brewery for £20,000. He died at the age of 49 in 1890.

Another member of The Scriveners' Company, who had a career which was perhaps rather less conventional than the lives of many of his colleagues, was Lewis Goldsmith, who joined the Company on 9 November 1809. He was both an attorney and a notary public, obtaining his notarial faculty on 5 January 1810 when he was about 46 years of age and after serving articles to a London notary named Martin Reynolds. Before entering legal practice he had spent some time in Poland as a journalist during the War of Independence there. Subsequently he lived in France where, by arrangement with Napoleon to whom he claimed to have been introduced by Talleyrand, he produced in 1802 a tri-weekly publication entitled *The Argus or London reviewed in Paris*. The following year he was imprisoned for refusing to print articles which criticised the British royal family. The French Government having attempted without success to exchange him for an important French prisoner held by the British, Goldsmith was sent by Bonaparte on a secret

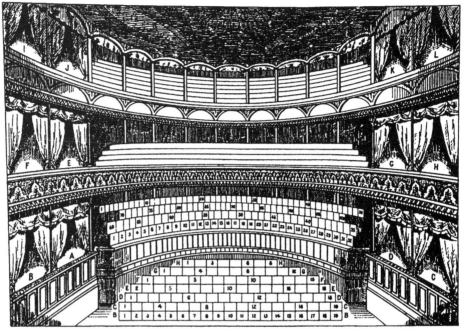

OPERA COMIQUE THEATRE.

MANAGER . . . . . MR. HARRY JACKSON.

PRICES OF ADMISSION.—PRIVATE BOXES, 21s. TO 63s.; STALLS, 10s.; DRESS CIRCLE, FIRST ROW, 6s.; SECOND AND THIRD ROWS, 5s.; CHAIRS (Bonnets allowed), 4s.; UPPER CIRCLE, 2s.6d.; AMPHITHEATRE, 1s.6d.; GALLERY, 1s.

DOORS OPEN AT 6.45, COMMENCE AT 7.15.

AT MR. MITCHELL'S ROYAL LIBRARY, 33, OLD BOND STREET,

Boxes, Orchestra Stalls, and Reserved Seats, in the most eligible positions, can always be secured for the Royal Italian Opera, all the Theatres, and every entertainment in London.

Tickets for the Royal Albert Hall, the Crystal Palace, also all Concerts and Flower Shows.

ROYAL LIBRARY, 33, OLD BOND STREET.

ALFRED HAYS, THE CITY BOX OFFICE, 4, ROYAL EXCHANGE BUILDINGS, CORNHILL, E.C.

Boxes, Stalls, and Reserved Seats, for both Operas and all Theatres, secured by Telegraphic and Telephonic Communication.

Tickets for all Concerts, Flower Shows, etc.   Season Tickets for the Crystal Palace.

Musicians for Evening and Dinner Parties. Programmes, etc., of the latest designs.

9   Playbill of the Opera Comique Theatre, London, mentioning Mitchell's Royal Library, owned by John Mitchell, Master of the Company, 1857-8.

mission to offer the Polish crown to Louis XVIII, then living in exile, on condition that Louis renounced his claim to the French throne. He escaped from France in 1809 on a ship bound for America and landed at Dover. It seems curious that, after all these adventures and an absence of some years from this country, he was able, within months of his return to England, to obtain his freedom of the Company and a notarial faculty, but presumably he had completed his articles with Martin Reynolds some years earlier while he was still in England. The law as a career does not seem to have appealed to him greatly since the only entry for him in a Law List occurs in 1810 when he was practising in Charlotte Street, Bloomsbury. Concentrating instead on his work as a political journalist he began the publication in 1811 of a journal entitled *The Anti-Gallican Monitor and Anti-Corsican Chronicle*, later known as *The British Monitor*. He also suggested that a public subscription should be raised for a price to be put on Napoleon's head and published a work entitled *Secret History of the Cabinet of Bonaparte*, followed the next year by a *Secret History of Bonaparte's Diplomacy*. In 1815 he published *An Appeal to the Governments of Europe on the Necessity of bringing Napoleon Bonaparte to Public Trial*. In 1825 he discontinued publication of his journal and returned to Paris, where he acted as 'Translator for the French Tribunal and Solicitor for the British Embassy'. He evidently established himself satisfactorily in Paris under the Bourbons and when Disraeli visited the city in 1842 gave a splendid banquet for him and also introduced him to his friends in the French political world. He died in Paris on 6 January 1846. His will was proved by his only surviving daughter, Georgina, who had become the second wife of the distinguished lawyer, Lord Lyndhurst, three times Lord Chancellor (1827-30, 1834-5 and 1841-6).

Music, the theatre and political journalism were not the only artistic and literary pursuits represented in The Scriveners' Company during the 19th century. Charles Robert Forrester, a London notary who joined the Company at the age of 21 in 1824 and succeeded to the notarial practice of his father at 5 North Gate, Royal Exchange, and was Master in 1842, was also a writer. His entry in the *Dictionary of National Biography* tells us that 'his profession afforded him abundant means, and he employed his money and his leisure in the pursuit of literature'. He was also 'a good classic and well acquainted with the Latin, French, German and Dutch languages. His writings, like his conversation, have a spontaneous flow of wit.' The first of these writings was a novel, *Castle Baynard or The Days of John*, which he published in 1824 under the pseudonym 'Hal Willis, student at law'. A second novel, which ran to four volumes and was entitled *Sir Roland, a Romance of the Twelfth Century*, appeared in 1827. In subsequent years he wrote many articles in magazines, several of which were published in two volumes in 1843 with the title *Phantasmagoria of Fun*. He died on 15 January 1850 at the age of 47.[22] His younger brother, Alfred Henry Forrester, also a member of the Company—he became a freeman in 1826—was a well-known artist who used the pseudonym, Alfred Crowquill. He exhibited at the Royal Academy in 1845 and 1846 and also contributed sketches to *Punch*. In addition he produced designs and effects for pantomimes,

10 'The Beauties of Brighton', watercolour by Alfred Crowquill.

illustrations for children's books and caricatures. In 1851 he modelled a statuette of the Duke of Wellington which he presented to Queen Victoria. Among his numerous publications, which he illustrated himself, were *Kindness and Cruelty*, or *The Grateful Ogre* (1859), *What Uncle Told Us* (1861) and *Dick Do-Little, The Idle Sparrow* (1870). He also produced the illustrations for many books written by authors other than himself. He died at his home in London on 26 May 1872.[23]

It would be interesting to know what part, if any, members of The Scriveners' Company, like Mitchell and Goldsmith, who were not based in the City of London, played in the Company's affairs. The Company itself, however, certainly played a part in the lives of members who had fallen on hard times. There are many entries in the account book 1733–1894 of payments of benevolences to freemen and liverymen of the Company or their widows or daughters who were in reduced circumstances. Mrs. Elizabeth Hughes, for instance, widow of the Company's beadle John Hughes, who was also a freeman of the Company, was paid a pension from

3 October 1800 to 13 October 1812. On 12 February 1813 the Company paid Thomas Stokes, then a Past Master and a member of the Court of Assistants, for her funeral. Charles Green, a notary and member of the Court of Assistants, received a Company pension from 17 November 1843 to 28 December 1848. This pension continued to be paid, after his death, to his widow whose funeral expenses were also borne by the Company in 1868.

A particularly sad situation requiring the Company's assistance was that of a notary named George Pyne Andrewes. Andrewes was born in Bristol in 1776, son of Thomas Andrewes, an attorney and notary public in that city. After qualifying as an attorney and notary he practised in Bristol for some years, moving to London about 1824, in which year he became a freeman of The Scriveners' Company and obtained a notarial faculty entitling him to practise in the area controlled by the Company. Initially the offices of his practice as an attorney and notary were in Birchin Lane, but by 1833 he was at 84 Lower Thames Street where he remained for over twenty years. His business must have declined, however, for in 1856 he was paid a benevolence by the Company. He died in Islington Workhouse at the age of 82 in 1857. If conditions in Victorian workhouses were distressing for the inmates they were certainly equalled by the state of the prisons at the time. Horsham Gaol was the melancholy abode on 12 October 1842 of Edward Hampton Noy, 'late of Bank House, Lower Lancing, Sussex, out of business, formerly a solicitor and notary public', who had become an insolvent debtor. After serving articles with his father, also a solicitor and notary but not a member of the Company, he practised for some years in Seething Lane but became bankrupt in 1829. He committed suicide in 1861, aged 59, at his home at Betchworth, Surrey, where there is a monument to him in the churchyard.

In the latter years of the 19th century there occurred an event in the history of The Scriveners' Company which must have concerned its members almost as much as the loss of the Case of the Free Scriveners over a hundred years earlier. This was the bankruptcy in 1885 for the sum of £800,000 of Alexander Ridgway, notary public and army agent, a past Master of the Company. He had practised in partnership in London with his father and his brother, Tobias Gainsford Ridgway (also a liveryman of the Company), for many years and had been Mayor of Dartmouth. When his bankruptcy occurred Ridgway had a house in Harley Street, an estate in Devon named Shepleigh Court and a seaside residence at Paignton named The Palace.[24] The Company's minute book records that on 25 January 1888 the Court of Assistants requested his resignation because of the bankruptcy. There is no evidence that this request was complied with and three years later, on 5 July 1891, Mr. Ridgway was found dead on the roadside at Warley Gap, near Brentwood, Essex. He was 65 years old and had died of cardiac failure. His estate amounted to £97.

8

THE TWENTIETH CENTURY:
A TIME OF GRADUAL EXPANSION

During the first half of the 20th century the affairs of The Scriveners' Company continued in much the same way as they had done during Victorian times. One of the Company's main concerns in this period related to the property which it owned in Noble Street. At the Court Meeting on 21 October 1909 the possibility of selling two of the houses, Nos. 12 and 13 Noble Street, which produced an annual rent of £250, was discussed, the figure envisaged being £4,000-£4,500. The Court decided not to sell the property but, instead, to rebuild the houses at a cost of £1,800-£2,000 and to let them at a higher rent—£300. However it would appear that these policies were less than successful since by 1913 the Court, at its meeting on 30 April, was again considering selling the properties. They were put up for auction on 10 March 1914 by the auctioneers Weatherall and Green. Henry Weatherall, a partner in this firm, was a member of the Company.[1] Unfortunately the properties failed to find a bidder but, as a result of the auction, the Company received an enquiry about a lease on 12 and 13 Noble Street and the properties were leased for 14 years to H.P. White Ltd. at a rent of £350 per annum, just two weeks before the outbreak of the First World War.[2]

At various points during the war years the Company made donations to appropriate causes. For example, at the meeting of the Court held on 28 July 1915 the Clerk reported that a cheque for £105 had been sent to the Belgian Lawyers Relief Fund, which had been set up to assist Belgian lawyers who had escaped from their country and settled in London. It was also a sign of the times, perhaps, that two years later, on 31 October 1917, the Court passed a resolution that no person who was not a natural born British subject should be admitted to the freedom. This decision was put to the test the following year when the Committee of Privileges, at its meeting on 31 July, had to consider the application for the freedom made by William Oswald Brown, the apprentice of Alexander Richard Cecil Ridgway, a London notary who was a member of the Company and a partner in the firm of John Venn & Sons, then of 75 and 77 Cornhill, and he was required to produce evidence of his nationality before his application for the freedom could be further considered. The matter of Mr Brown's application was considered again at a number of subsequent meetings, and it was not until the Court meeting held on 25 January 1922 that Mr. Brown, having obtained a certificate of naturalisation under the Aliens Act 1914, was admitted to the freedom of the Company by servitude preparatory to applying for a faculty to act as a notary public. He duly obtained his faculty and practised as a notary for many years, dying in 1958 at the age of 91.

During the first part of the century the Company continued to make donations to suitable causes and to assist relations of deceased members who had fallen on hard times. In 1907, for instance, £100 was contributed to the preservation of Crosby Hall and in the following year the Company gave 25 guineas to the London Hospital and £100 to the Winchester Cathedral Restoration Fund. In 1908 the death occurred of Miss Louisa Loveday, a pensioner of the Company and daughter of a freeman named Samuel Loveday who had been proprietor of a pawnbroking business in Gray's Inn Road. The Court decided on 27 January 1909 that her annual pension of £40 should be continued in favour of her sister. During these years and subsequently addresses of condolence were sent to the Royal Family on the deaths of Queen Victoria,

11   Portrait of Joshua Dawson Watts, notary public and Master of the Company 1913-4, 1932-3.

King Edward VII, Queen Alexandra, King George V, Queen Mary and King George VI. The sum of £52 10s. 0d. was contributed to the Fund for the Memorial to Queen Victoria by decision of the Court made on 30 April 1901. The letter of condolence to Queen Alexandra and the Royal Family after the death of King Edward VII was acknowledged on 3 August 1910 by Winston Churchill, who was then Home Secretary.

In the years between the two World Wars there were additions to the Company's assets in the form of presentations from members. On 28 October 1925 the Master, John Dalton Venn, presented the Company at the Court Dinner held on that date with a silver rosewater dish to commemorate his family's long connection with the Scriveners' and to record the fact that his great-grandfather, the first John Venn, had been Master one hundred years previously. In 1929 the notary Edwin Courtney Walker gave to the Company a badge to be used by the Clerk. At the Court Meeting held on 29 January 1930 it was resolved that the Master's badge be repaired and the chain lengthened at a cost of £60 10s. 0d. and that the names of past Masters be engraved on the shields of the chains. At the meeting of the Court held on 30 October 1935 it was reported that John Thomas Atkinson, a solicitor and notary

12   Scriveners' Company painted silk banner unveiled at Painters' Hall, 30 January 1986.[3]

public practising at Selby, Yorkshire, who, in addition to being Upper Warden of the Company in 1909 (the year of his death), was also President of the Yorkshire Law Society and Honorary Secretary of the Society of Provincial Notaries Public of England and Wales, had left £100 to the Company for the purchase in his memory of 'a piece of plate or a mace or some article of an artistic nature'. It was decided that a salt be purchased and that the base of it should bear the Company's arms. The ancient practice of masters of apprentice scriveners presenting the Company with a silver spoon upon each apprentice's completion of servitude seems to have ceased in the late 17th century, but during the later years of the 20th century other items (usually of silver) were presented so that at the present day the Company has an interesting stock of artefacts. The Company's silver includes the Beadle's mace, thought to be the oldest in the City, which was presented to the Company in 1670 at the time of Sir Robert Clayton's mastership by George Perryer, the Upper Warden, who became Master in 1674. In March 1996 Ian Pickford from the popular television series, 'Antiques Road Show', was invited to view them and give his comments, and photographs taken on that occasion are reproduced here.

13 Ian Pickford with items of the Company's silver, March 1996.

14 Further items of the Company's silver,
March 1996.

In 1931 there was a discussion at the January meeting of the Court about the possibility of purchasing the Hall of The Coachmakers' Company. It was resolved that a committee be appointed to interview the Clerk of The Coachmakers' Company to ascertain the Coachmakers' views on this idea. On 29 April 1931 the Clerk reported to the Court 'the result of the interview'. As the Scriveners' minutes make no further reference to this proposal it cannot have been received by the Coachmakers with any enthusiasm. In fact, that Company wrote to the Scriveners later the same year asking what price they might ask for their properties 12/13 and 14/15 Noble Street. These properties, since the war, were becoming something of a burden to the Company. Nos.12 and 13 had suffered a fire in 1922 and two years later the lessees, H.P. White Ltd., had gone into liquidation, a new lease being granted to a firm named Joynson & Co. at a rent of £375 per annum. At 14 and 15 Noble Street the lessees, Messrs. F.H. Searl, were in arrears with their rent. Consideration was therefore given to the approach of The Coachmakers' Company and the Clerk was instructed by the Building Committee of The Scriveners' Company to reply to them saying that an offer which would produce £14,000 net after payment of the expenses of sale would be considered, subject to confirmation by the Court. By 26 October 1932 Messrs. F.H. Searl owed the Company £96 17s. 6d. in rent for 14 and 15 Noble Street so the Scriveners repossessed the premises in April of the following year. The premises appear to have remained empty until all the Company's property in Noble Street was destroyed in an air raid on 29 December 1940. At the Court meeting held on 28 January 1948 it was reported that the Company had received £1,699 from the War Damage Commission for 14 and 15 Noble Street. The building on the site of the Company's Hall at Shelley House, Noble Street, was demolished in the late 1990s and a new office block has been erected on the site.

During the war the Scriveners had again been giving thought to the idea of purchasing a site for a Hall and offices. On 26 July 1944 the Court considered a letter from the estate agents Weatherall, Green & Smith about a site on the banks of the Thames but it was resolved at that time to take no further action. In January 1951 the surveyors Richard Ellis & Co. were instructed to undertake a survey of the Noble Street property and in July the Court was informed that negotiations were in progress for it to be sold to The Coachmakers' Company. At the October Court in that year the members were told that the Coachmakers were trying to persuade other Livery Companies to join in the purchase of the property. Weatherall, Green & Smith, however, advised the Company to serve notice on the City Corporation to purchase compulsorily. In 1952 the Coachmakers offered £9,000 for the property, which was accepted. Two years later no contracts had been exchanged and the City Corporation issued a compulsory purchase notice, whereupon the Coachmakers withdrew their offer. On 31 October 1956 the Court was informed that the Corporation had agreed on a figure of £16,350 for compulsory purchase. The sale was completed in 1957. At the Court meeting held at Tallow Chandlers' Hall on 30 April 1958, the question of a Livery Hall for those companies not having one was discussed by the Scriveners. The Master (Frederick Campbell Giles, a notary and partner in H. de Pinna & John Venn) said that there was shortly to be an opening ceremony of the Livery Hall and ancillary accommodation in the new Guildhall office block. A member of the Court, Herbert Sutton Syrett, who was a solicitor in the City, said that these premises were intended for Companies which did not have their own Halls. They would accommodate between 100 and 150 people. The Clerk was asked to make further enquiries, but nothing transpired. At a Court meeting held on 3 May 1972 the Master, Joseph Jenkins, proposed that the Company should again consider the possibility of acquiring its own Hall. He said that one of the guests at the dinner had promised £1,000 towards the cost. A New Hall Committee was set up to take the matter further and to consider the possibility of acquiring a Hall in a larger property development. Various sites were suggested, including a redundant City church and a barge moored within the City's boundaries. Unfortunately, however, it seems that the enormous increase in London property prices during the last 28 years has made the acquisition of a Hall for the Company an impractical proposition.

In the later years of the century there was a considerable increase in the social activities of the Company. For very many years these had consisted largely of the two dinners held traditionally in the spring and the autumn and known as the Livery Dinner and the Ladies' Dinner. Indeed the requirement for two dinners per year was first prescribed in the Company's Charter in 1617: 'there shall be one dinner for the Master, Wardens and Assistants of the said Society and other the freemen of the same Company to be kept yearly upon the day of the election of the new Master and Wardens, and the other for the Master, Wardens, Assistants and Livery of the said Company yearly to be kept on the day when the Lord Mayor takes his oath at Westminster'.

Shortly after his appointment to the Court, John Phillips QC submitted a paper in which he drew attention to the small number of social activities that currently took place and suggested that attempts be made to add to them for the greater benefit of the Company and its members. This gave rise to the introduction of monthly lunches, then at very modest cost, and these proved popular. A reception to follow the election and installation of the new officers in the summer was also instituted and this continues to be well supported.

There have been innovations in other directions as well. The Lord Mayor is provided with a quill pen to use when signing his Declaration at the Silent Ceremony at the commencement of his year of office. The quill is then retrieved, a silver commemorative plaque is attached, and the quill pen re-presented at a lunch traditionally taking place at the Mansion House early in December. At the same time a Parker Duofold pen with the Company's coat of arms engraved upon the cap or decal is also given by the kind offices of the Parker Pen Company. This practice was first started during the mastership of Robert Urquhart in December 1983. A similar presentation is made to the Sheriffs at a reception in January, and we reproduce a photograph taken at the presentation made in January 1999. These traditions have become established and now make a modest but noteworthy addition to the annual diary of events both for the Lord Mayor and the Sheriffs which is much appreciated by them.

Anthony Burgess, the senior partner of Cheeswrights and Master of the Company in 1969, kept alive the literary traditions of Charles and Alfred Forrester and John Mitchell by writing two finely illustrated books on *The Notary in Opera* (1995) and *The Notary and other Lawyers in Gilbert and Sullivan* (1997).

Another interesting development in the history of the Company during the latter part of the 20th century has been the inclusion in its membership of officers of the College of Arms, archivists and librarians. The first modern member of the College to become a Scrivener was James Arnold Frere, then Bluemantle Pursuivant of Arms, later Chester Herald, who became a freeman and a liveryman of the Company in 1949. However, as Dr. Steer noted in Volume 1, there was an historical precedent for this in the person of Sir William Segar, Garter King of Arms 1604-1633 who was 'bred a scrivener'.

In 1953, Colin Cole, who was at that time Fitzalan Pursuivant of Arms Extraordinary (and later Portcullis Pursuivant), acquired his freedom and livery. He became Windsor Herald of Arms in 1966, and in 1978 was appointed Garter Principal King of Arms, an office which he held until 1992, being knighted KCVO (1983) and KCB (1992). Also in 1978 he served as Master of The Scriveners' Company and has continued as a highly respected member of the Court of Assistants to this day. Sir Colin served as Sheriff of the City of London 1976-77. His son, Giles, is also a liveryman and a member of the Court of Assistants.

John Brooke-Little, Bluemantle Pursuivant of Arms, became a freeman and liveryman in April 1958. He was Richmond Herald 1967-80, Norroy and Ulster King of Arms 1980-95 and Clarenceux King of Arms 1995-7. He was created CVO in 1984 and became Master of the Company in 1985. He has been an influential figure in heraldic circles particularly through his editorship of *The Coat of Arms*, a quarterly magazine published by the Heraldry Society, which he founded in 1947.

Other members of the Company who were heralds were Francis Steer (Maltravers Herald Extrordinary), Rodney Dennys (Somerset Herald), George Squibb QC (Norfolk Herald Extraordinary); and Peter Gwynn-Jones, an Honorary Liveryman, is the current Garter Principal King of Arms. Another herald to be admitted to The Scriveners' Company was Michael Maclagan, who became a freeman and liveryman of the Company in 1959 when he was Slains Pursuivant to the Lord High Constable of Scotland. He was appointed Portcullis Pursuivant in 1970 and Richmond Herald in 1980. He became Master in 1988. During his mastership, Lady Thatcher, who was then Prime Minister, became a Freeman of the City of London and was presented by the Company with a quill pen which she used on her admission. We reproduce a photograph both of Lady Thatcher signing her Declaration and of the letter of thanks sent by her to the Master. A number of the current members of the Company have interests in heraldic matters without being heralds themselves, and an annual donation is made by the Company to the Heraldry Society, which presents an annual lecture in honour of the Company.

15 Lady Thatcher (then Margaret Thatcher), Prime Minister, signing the Freedom Register of the City, 26 May 1989.

A particularly prominent and popular member of the Company in the years after the Second World War was Gerald Henderson, Sub-Librarian and Keeper of the Muniments of St Paul's Cathedral. He became a freeman and liveryman in 1945 and Master in 1956. When he died in 1962 he left several bequests and half the residue of his estate to the Company. The bequests consisted of his Past Master's badge, various precious stones to be set in the Master's jewel and his framed photograph of the pen and its ink stand presented by the Company to the Queen at her Coronation. The other half of the residue was bequeathed to the College of Arms and Sir Colin Cole was Gerald Henderson's Executor. Gerald Henderson also made an appointment in his will of various settled funds, expressing the wish that they be used to augment any amount which was to be spent in entertainment arranged for the Company's pleasure. A toast to his memory is drunk annually at the Company's Livery Dinner. One of Henderson's colleagues was David Floyd Ewin, the Registrar and Receiver of St Paul's

1O DOWNING STREET
LONDON SW1A 2AA

THE PRIME MINISTER   31 July 1989

Dear Mr. Maclagan,

    I was so sorry to hear that my busy programme on 26 May
prevented The Scriveners Company from presenting me with the
quill pen used during the Freedom Ceremony. However I am
absolutely delighted that you have now sent this to me. It
looks magnificent in its beautiful blue presentation box and
I would be extremely grateful if you could convey my sincere
thanks to all members of your Company.

    To be granted the Freedom of the City of London was a
very great honour and your kind gift will serve forever as a
reminder of that most memorable and historic day in my life.

    With renewed thanks and warmest good wishes,

Yours sincerely

Margaret Thatcher

Michael Maclagan, Esq., C.V.O.

16 Letter from Lady Thatcher to Michael Maclagan (then Master), dated 31 July 1989.

Cathedral, who was Master of The Scriveners' Company in 1961 and was later knighted for his services to the Cathedral.

In the last 50 years the Company has continued to receive into its ranks many other professional people. Indeed, the Court of Assistants has borne in mind the importance of maintaining the Scriveners' tradition of being a Livery Company which particularly welcomes members of the professions rather than captains of industry, although not to the latter's exclusion. This is evidenced by the fact that amongst the current members of the Company is Sir Ernest Harrison, chairman of Racal over many years, and it is to be noted that the enormously successful Vodafone company started its life within the Racal group of companies before being floated separately not many years ago. The number of women in the Company has grown and today there are three lady members of the Court, including Sylvia Tutt who was the first woman to become Master of a City Livery Company, The Chartered Secretaries and Administrators' Company, in 1985.

In addition to the notaries and solicitors who for so long constituted the backbone of the Company, chartered accountants and chartered secretaries have also become members. Leonard Harman, a chartered accountant, was Master in 1980, and his son James, also a chartered accountant, was Clerk of the Company from 1981 to 1994 and then Master in 1995. A notable chartered secretary was John Phillips who has been mentioned above. In addition to becoming Master of The Scriveners' Company in 1982, he founded two other livery companies, the Chartered Secretaries and Administrators in 1977 and the Arbitrators in 1981, and served as Master of both Companies.

1973 was the year of the Company's 600th anniversary and the Master was Adrian Orchard, a notary and partner in De Pinna Scorer & John Venn. An exhibition of scrivening was mounted at Reed House, Piccadilly which was described in its programme as being an exhibition of the Scriveners' treasures, and it contained 'examples of calligraphy both ancient and modern'. It was opened on 2 October by Princess Alexandra. The Ladies Dinner that year took place at the Mansion House and Lord Denning recalled in his speech at the Dinner that scriveners would have been responsible for the writing of Magna Carta. The Scriveners' Play—*The Incredulity of St Thomas*—was performed on 28 November at the Church of St Martin-within-Ludgate in the presence of the Lord Mayor. There was also a reception at the College of Arms and Francis Steer's *History* was published. The press were enthusiastic about these various activities. 'Anyone planning to celebrate a 600th anniversary might take a lesson from the Worshipful Company of Scriveners on how to do it', wrote one; and Philip Howard wrote in *The Times*: 'The scriveners of Britain are celebrating the 600th anniversary of their ancient, elegant and flourishing craft'. In addition, the Company's Sexcentenary Charity Fund was established in that year, and has since then been the basis for the Company's annual charitable grants to medical, welfare and educational causes.

Since the passing of 'The Act concerning Peter's Pence and Dispensations' in 1533, notaries in England and Wales have received their faculties from the

17 Dr. George Carey, Archbishop of Canterbury, and others on his admission as a freeman, 17 April 1997.

Archbishop of Canterbury. The Company therefore decided in 1975, in view of the close connection of the London notaries with the Scriveners, to invite Lord Ramsey who, as Dr Michael Ramsey, had been the 100th Archbishop, to become an Honorary Freeman and Liveryman of the Company, this being the first occasion that an admission to the Honorary Freedom and Livery had taken place since 1666. Lord Ramsey was duly admitted to the Company in October 1975 and he and Lady Ramsey attended the Ladies Dinner which followed the meeting of the Court of Assistants. The present Archbishop of Canterbury, Dr George Carey, was likewise admitted as an Honorary Freeman and Liveryman and simultaneously admitted as a Freeman of the City of London in April 1997 in a memorable ceremony in the Court Room of HQS Wellington, presided over by the Master, and attended by the Lord Mayor and Sheriffs and the Town Clerk and Chamberlain of the City of London. The Master in question was Barry O'Meara, a solicitor, whose father, Desmond, was Honorary Clerk of the Company between 1974 and 1981.

At the meeting of the Court held in July 1982 it was resolved that the Guild Church of St Martin-within-Ludgate should be adopted as the Company's official

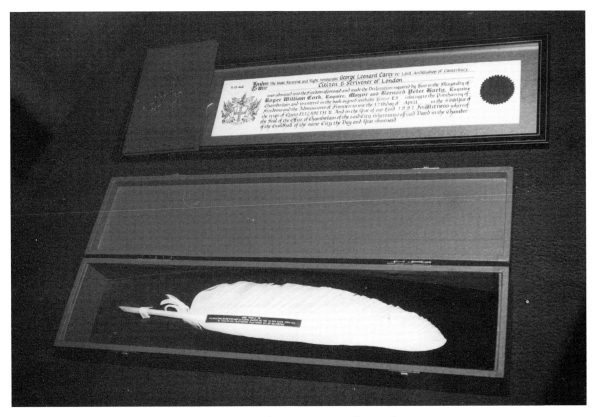

18 A Scriveners' presentation quill in its box.

church, and a popular annual Carol Service takes place there in December conducted by the Company's Honorary Chaplain, the Rev. Philip Buckler, who has given some meditations which have been well received. At the same meeting of the Court it was resolved that the honorary freedom of The Scriveners' Company should be granted to Don Vicente Font Boix, a notary of Barcelona, with whom notarial members of the Company had had many fruitful contacts. He was presented with his freedom and an illuminated address at the Court meeting on 19 January of the following year. In subsequent years other European notaries have been similarly honoured, namely, from Paris, Bertrand Hohl in 1977 and Paul Chardon in 1999, and from Bari, Vittorio di Cagno in 1999. The links of the scrivener notaries with their counterparts in Europe and elsewhere have been cemented by their admission to membership of the Union Internationale du Notariat Latin which took place in October 1998. This momentum towards consolidation of the international aspects of notarial practice was foreshadowed in July 1930 when the Court resolved to adopt a recommendation of the Examination Committee that,

19 Sheriffs Gavyn Arthur and Brian Harris, with the then Upper Warden, Neil Grimston, and their presentation quill pens, January 1999.

there was no objection to masters permitting their apprentices to reside for a period not exceeding two years abroad for the purpose of learning the foreign language in which the apprentice proposes to qualify with a view to applying for admission to the Freedom of the Company for the purpose of practising as a Notary.

Several articled clerks were subsequently sent by their notarial masters in London to study in France, Spain or elsewhere on the Continent. In January 1963 the Court discussed the question of the apprenticeship to a member of the Company of a Spanish national and agreed that there was no objection to non-British nationals being accepted as apprentices.

An eminent member of the Company in an appropriate field is Donald Jackson, who joined the Company in 1973 when he was chairman of the Society of Scribes and Illuminators. He became Master in 1997. He is one of the leading calligraphers and is currently engaged on a project to produce the first new illuminated Bible for 500 years. An article in *The Times* newspaper appeared in March 1999 featuring him and his project, and we have been authorised to reproduce the photograph of him working on his project. During his year as Master he was able to point the Company in the direction of colleges offering courses in calligraphy to which donations could

20 Past Master Donald Jackson at work on his bible project, from *The Times*, 9 March 1999.

10 DOWNING STREET
LONDON SW1A 2AA

THE PRIME MINISTER   11 March 1999

Dear Andrew,

Thank you for your letter of 11 February, in which you invited me to join you in resisting the Lord Chancellor's proposals to abolish the monopoly which the Company has over notarial work in central London. I should explain that the Lord Chancellor's proposals are not his alone; they represent the agreed policy of the Government as a whole.

In the course of reviewing the monopoly, the Lord Chancellor sought the views of interested parties, including the Scriveners' Company, and considered them carefully before coming to a decision. The arguments that you now raise in favour of preservation of the monopoly were taken into account during that review.

I note your argument that Scrivener notaries offer a specialist service, which is of value to the City of London as an international trading centre. Allowing non-Scrivener notaries to practise in central London would, in your view, dilute the level of expertise in the City, and thereby undermine the respect in which London notaries are held. I should emphasise that the Government's proposals will not prevent notaries from being members of the Scriveners' Company if they wish, and will not prevent notaries from advertising their adherence to the Company, if they believe that is a guarantee of higher quality. Those clients who want the specialist services which your members provide will

- 2 -

be able to obtain them. However, the Government's Conclusion is that your argument does not justify the statutory prevention of non-Scrivener notaries from offering their services to those who might want them within central London.

Yours sincerely,
Tony Blair

Andrew Hill Esq

21 Letter to the Company from Tony Blair, Prime Minister, re the Access to Justice Bill, 11 March 1999.

usefully be made for the encouragement of such students, and these donations continue. He also produced and presented to the Company the framed calligraphic rendition of the lists of Masters and Clerks that hang in HQS Wellington adjacent to the Clerk's office, and which were unveiled by the Duke of Norfolk, Earl Marshal, in June 1996.

The notarial members of the Company in the latter years of the 20th century received increasing criticism for the continuing existence of their exclusive jurisdiction to practise in the City of London and its environs. Concern arose during the passage of the bills leading to the Courts and Legal Services Act 1990 and the Competition Act 1998 that that jurisdiction would be affected, but at that time the suggested changes were successfully resisted. However, the jurisdiction was finally removed by the Access to Justice Act 1999 despite spirited resistance from the Company's supporters in the House of Commons, notably Peter Brooke M.P., and Sir Nicholas Lyell M.P. The Company's position was that Scrivener Notaries have special qualifications and knowledge. They not only have to pass the examinations which apply to notaries elsewhere in the country, but also to undergo a period of apprenticeship with a City firm of notaries and

JOHN VENNS ~ NOTARIES IN LONDON

John Venn
1778 - 1856

John Sise Venn
1810 - 1857

John Venn
1839 - 1902

John Dalton Venn
1868 -

John Venn
1899 -

22 Portraits of five generations of the Venn family, notaries public and Masters of the Scriveners' Company.

to pass examinations testing knowledge of two languages and familiarity with foreign law and practice. As a result, Scrivener Notaries are qualified to read, translate and advise on foreign legal documents, and such qualifications and knowledge are greatly valued by those working in the international business environment in the City. However, the Lord Chancellor was unmoved by this argument and he pressed ahead with his proposed reform on the basis that, if the Scrivener Notaries' argument was correct, they should thrive in the new competitive environment. At one point the Clerk wrote to all lawyer members of the House of Commons including the Prime Minister, Tony Blair, in an attempt to enlist their support, and the Prime Minister's letter in reply supporting his Lord Chancellor is reproduced.

1998 was the year of the Company's 625th anniversary, and the Master, Oliver Kinsey, a solicitor, arranged for a specially inscribed enamel box bearing the arms of the Company to be commissioned from Halcyon Days for the occasion. He also traced Sir David Clayton Bt., the 12th Baronet and collateral descendant of Sir Robert Clayton, the Company's first Master to become Lord Mayor,[4] and the Company was delighted to admit Sir David as an Honorary Freeman at a Court Meeting on HQS Wellington in October 1999.

Affiliations with the armed forces have been established, firstly with HMS *Beaver*, a type 22 Frigate, and secondly with LXX Squadron of the Royal Air Force, based at RAF Lyneham. In each case an annual donation was made for the welfare fund of these establishments. HMS *Beaver* was commissioned in 1984 and her first commander, Sir John Lang, became an Honorary Freeman of the Company at a Court Meeting held in January 1986. Sadly, HMS *Beaver* was decommissioned in February 1999, but a replacement affiliation with a new type 23 Frigate, namely HMS *Portland* (now being built in Glasgow in the former Yarrow's shipyard), has been arranged, and her commissioning is due to take place in May 2001. LXX Squadron, which flies Hercules aircraft, has been active in the Falklands, the Gulf War, Bosnia and Kosovo, and wherever drops of military personnel, equipment, food and medical supplies are required. In both cases the affiliation has been pleasing to the recipients who have welcomed members of the Company to voyages and Open Days respectively and whom we have been pleased to welcome to our dinners.

It can therefore be seen that the Company is increasingly active in a number of spheres whilst retaining its traditional links with its core trades and professions, such as the notarial profession and calligraphy, to which can now be added the links referred to with the heraldic profession.

The Worshipful Company of Scriveners is proud of its history and looks forward with confidence to the maintenance of its position as a unique organisation in the City of London.

Appendix I
MAYOR'S REMEMBRANCER ROLLS

Some biographical material on early scriveners is to be found among the records of the City Remembrancer who was responsible for recording matters brought before the Court of the Lord Mayor for summary judgement.

(Roll A 29 Membrane 1) In a list of diverse men adjudicated to prison in the time of Nicholas Twyford, knight, mayor, 28 Aug 1389 is John Whyte, *lymenour*, who was committed to prison for a debt of 16s which Henry Gaysle, *scriveyn*, recovered against him on the award of the masters of the *Lymenours*, and for 40d which the court adjudged that he should pay to the chamberlain for disobeying the ordinances of his mistery.

(Membrane 1b, 23 Jan 1389) Whereas diverse charters of diverse misteries, granted to them by the king and his progenitors, had in the time of Nicholas Brembre, knight, been taken into the Chamber of the Guildhall into the custody of Richard Odyham, chamberlain.

(Footnote 3) During the first mayoralty of Nicholas Brembre, 21 March 1377, to 13 Oct 1378, the Common Council ordered that all masters of misteries should bring in their charters for the governance of their misteries to the mayor and chamberlain. *Cal. of Letter Book H*, p.193. Unwin *Gilds of London*, p.156, regards this as aimed against the manufacturing guilds, but it appears to have applied to all the misteries, and was probably a move.

(Roll A 32 Membrane 3, 12 Mar 1393) Marion Stock, having complained that John Ruddok, a text-scriveyn[er], to whom her son John had been apprentice for eight years, had withdrawn himself from the liberty of the City [of London] and did not support or instruct the apprentice and John Newent, cordwainer, William Broun, chandler, Thomas Burton, fuller, and other neighbours having given evidence to the same effect, the boy was exonerated from his apprenticeship. According to Unwin *Gilds of London* (pp.167 & 370-1), the text-writers of ordinary book-hand, as distinguished from the writers of the court-hand, were two separate crafts, even as late as 1422.

(Roll A 35 Membrane 2b, 30 Nov 1395) The ship *Seinte Mariknyght* was sold by Henry Sanday of Lucca, a burgess of Venice and owner and master of the ship, to Gilbert Maghfeld, a merchant of London, 'according to the Law of Olyron'. At the request of the vendor the Deed of Sale was sealed with the Mayoralty Seal for better evidence and security and marked with the accustomed mark of one Martin Seman, papal and imperial notary.[1]

(Roll A 40 Membrane 6, 17 Aug 1409) Francis Marini, a merchant of Florence, asked that three open letters from the Priors of Florence, sealed with their seals, might be enrolled in the Memoranda Rolls of the City of London. The mayor and aldermen ordered the documents to be entered. They concern powers of attorney and there was a certificate entered dated 28 June 1409 from the Priors of the Arts and the Standard Bearer of Justice that Firence Pieri Teci was a public and authentic notary and that his documents were worthy of credit in public and private within and without courts of justice.

(Roll A 42 Membrane 1, 26 Mar 1412) There were certificates of Robert Northelod, clerk of the Diocese of Wells and a public notary, procurator general of the Court of Canterbury and of William Bray, clerk, of the Diocese of Lincoln, public notary, present when William Briggenorth late apprentice of John Cosseham, mercer, admitting errors in his behaviour.

(Roll A 73 Membrane 6) Is a notarial document drawn up by William Brampton, clerk, of the Diocese of York, notary by imperial authority in 1447.

Appendix II

'A Character of a London Scrivener'[1]

A London Scrivener is a Creature begot by a Pen, and hatcht up in an Ink-pot. Leſſer ſtuff ſerves to his production, then to a Country Pedler's : the wing of a Gooſe ſets up forty of them. His Gown is curs'd to a perpetual Autumn, hence 'tis ever bare, and has as little wooll upon it, as if at next remove it were to be made Parchment; his Eares hang on like rotten fruit, the leaſt unkind blaſt of a Paſſenger blows them off; his Ink is Poyſon had it neither Gall nor Copprice; he looks like the by blow of a Country Attorny, from whom he differs as a Botcher does from a Taylor. The Attorny may have the honour to go to Hell on horſe-back, while the baſe knave fairly foots it after him. With relation to the Common-wealth he is a neceſſary Evil, without whom men would grow honeſt and friends, and then the Body Politick muſt needs fall, being no longer compounded of different Elements and Humours. Better Schollers there are many, but few greater Writers : and thoſe that have curſed the Invention of the Preſs for others ſakes, may more juſtly do the ſame to that of the Pen for his. I should gueſs his Trade of very great Antiquity, ſince I read God made Indentures of Covenant with Adam, but that we know Adam had no money, and the Scrivener would not do it Gratis. Beſide, had God made Scriveners, he would never have pronounced of the ſeven days work, that all was good. Had Scriveners bin in the old World, it had ſaved the Deluge, and accurſed Mankind had deſtroyed one another. A ſurreptitious race of men, not of Gods Creation, but born (like Vermin) out of the corruption of ſeveral Ages, or (like ſome Africk Monſters) the Amphibious product of a Heterogeneous Copulation : for when Perſons of different Intereſts and humours met together in a Contract, this Jarring Conjunction begat Scriveners, who at firſt (Viper-like) devoured their Parents, and have ever ſince (like a Wolf in the ſide) gnaw'd their Livelyhood out of the bowells of thoſe they hang upon. Methinks they ſhould be banished all well governed Kingdoms; or at leaſt (like Jews in Italy) wear a mark of diſtinction about them, like perſons that dwell in Infected houſes, that endangered Paſſengers may ſee and avoid them. Where they once get in, they ſpread like the Itch, and become as universal as the Sickneſs; had a Scrivener been among the Iſraelites, there need no other puniſhment to have forced them out of Egypt. They themſelves had bin the greateſt Plague, and Pharoah would have fled, not purſued them into the bottom of the Sea. A Generation of men able to enter into the Devil, the onely thing more unſatiate than Hell : ſome men pretend to fear and honour them, but 'tis as men Court their Hangman, for a more favourable Execution; or as the Indians Worship the Devil and the Spaniard, that they may do them the leſs harm. When he is examining an Eſtate, you would imagine him caſting its water to find what diſeaſe it labours of, and to be ſure (like a Knaviſh Chirurgeon) he will either find a Cure of it, or make one. Sometimes he playes the Baud, proſtitutes the ſame Title to all commers, and (if you ſee him ſoundly) will not ſtick to Mortgage the ſame Eſtate for you to ſeven ſeveral Perſons : ſometimes he folders up a crackt Title, and paſſes it away for a pure Maiden head; if it be weak, he dares ſtrengthen it by Forgery; and ſecure but his Ears, his man and he (two Knights o'th' Poſt) ſhall out ſwear the Devil. If you would make a ſafe Purchaſe, you muſt ſpend half the value of your Land in ſearching the Title : then he tells you, your Eſtate is ſecured, that is the beſt part of it to himſelf. But all the flaws he finds in the Title, may be ſtopt up with money from the adverſe party : if both ſee him ſoundly, then, that he may deal equally between man and man, he makes them alike miſerable, drawing the conveyances on either ſide ſo weak, and yet ſo ſtrong, that neither party ſhall have the advantage, but both endeavouring to recover what each knows to be his own, and to be neithers, they at laſt waſte away their Eſtates (like a Snowball) with handling it, ſpend double the purchaſe-money to ſecure the Land, and the Usurers (to end the ſtrife) ſieze on that which each of them have Mortgaged, and neither can redeem. Then the Uſurers part ſtakes; and ſo lim and canton out a brave Eſtate, (like Alexanders Empire) into petty Lordſhips. If he deale in mony, his Uſurer and he, are like the Hunter and his Dog; (or to ſpeak in their own Phraſe) they anſwer each other, as the Counter-part and Original Indenture : then (like the Devil) he walks up and down ſeeking whom he may devour : does his beſt endeavour to make you poor, that you may be forc't for ſupply to him, who is the laſt remedy, and indeed worſe than the diſeaſe. If you would borrow, he marches to your Neighbours, enquiring into your Eſtate, and ſmelling at your Reputation, ſpoyling your good name to gain you credit. He is for maintaining old Cuſtomes, and (among the reſt) for that of ten in the hundred, and what now a dayes bate the Uſurer, you must pay the Scrivener. If his Uſurer and he chance to ſtart a young Heir, he is employed, like the Hound, to purſue the Game, which he never leaves till he hath given him a Mortal gripe : then like the Lyon and the Jackall they divide the Prey; the Uſurer gnaws off all the fleſh, and the Scrivener picks the bones. To ſtirke the greater terrour into the Novice, he ſeats himſelf in all his Formalities, his furr'd Cap and Gown, his Pen in one Ear (if both be not off for Forgery) in the mid'ſt of a company of Writings, the Caſes of fo many undone perfons, a fight worfe than the Gallowes, able to extort Confeffion without the help of a Wrack, compofing his Countenance after the graveft Mode, dreadfully ridiculous, and moft Majeftically fimple, when after a tedious harangue (like a Dog making a circle before he lies down) of the ill fortune of thofe young men which fall into the hands of Knavifh Scriveners, (where he reads him his own Doom in the third Perfon) and of his happinefs in lighting on him (where to underftand him rightly, he muft read him backwards) telling him how defirous he is of his profperity, feeing to hang upon him to prevent his ruine, (when 'tis as a weight hangs on a Clock, to drive him on fafter; (or as an Angler, feeming to draw away the baite, that he may the more greedily take it) at laft he falls upon that he hath moft mind to, his eftate : Defires him to deal plainly, and lay open his cafe, as a fick man does to his Phyfitian, that he may the better Cure him, whereas 'tis really like the Baring a man's breaft to his Enemy, that he may the furer wound him : while my Youngfter, not daring to do otherwife, deals (God knows) very fimply and honeftly : the Scrivener mean time, like an Inquifitor, ftretching him upon the Wrack, writing down his Confeffion, out of all which he draws up a Sentence, mifcalled a Bond or a Conveyance : and when he hath wound him up to the higheft pag, and perceives him pumpt quite dry, he lets him down, prefents him a paper, makes him Sign and Seal the Warrant of his own Execution : and then by Law Condemns and Executes him. This unmerciful Thief robs the very Beggar, and fticks not to pick a Courtiers pocket, though he knows 'tis the Kings mony. He is fo ftrict a Profecutor of Juftice, that he maintains it beyond the utmoft rigour ; ftretches Juftice her felf upon the wrack, and upon an hours failure, feizes more then the forfeiture. He prays for Non-performance of the Condition, that he may take the advantage of the Penalty : and exceeds fo far in Cruelty, that curfed Jew, that he will have not the flefh alone, but the blood too. When you have incurr'd a forfeiture, he tells you the exactnefs of the Law, and to be fecure from the Ufurer, you muft compound with the Scrivener, and almoft pay the Penalty to be freed from it. But when he has Bound you never fo faft, for mony he will Releafe you; teach you to evade the Articles himfelf compofed, content fo he may be a Knave, to prove no Scrivener. Thus he plays faft and loofe, breaths hot and cold, and the fame Devil that binds the Charms, unties them too. 'Tis a pretty fight to fee them running about the Exchange, fmelling at the Merchants, juft like Dogs, fawning upon fome, and biting others. If any be in his Books, he fticks to him like a Remora, a fufficient Lett to his weightieft affairs; and while his Veffel fuffers Shipwrack abroad, he himfelf fplits on a more dangerous Rock, enchanted by thefe Syrens at home. A Plague worfe then Pirates, Shipwrack it felf cannot fave you from them : your very Convoyes (your fureties) protect you not from them, but fecure you the fafter to them. No mony, which fecures you from a Thief, will not fave you from him : he is one mifery after the very laft, the caufe of our ruine and the effect too : when all other miffortunes have deftroyed us , he follows as a referve, and after Execution quarters us. When all the World has fhaken you off, he fiezes you: Lice and Scriveners ftick faft unto you when you are beggard. If a man wade innocently into the muddy ftreams of Suretyfhip, he is fuddenly feiz'd by thefe Leeches, which once fattened, will never leave fucking till he faint, or they burft and die. He has a great ftroke at killing men; a miferable comforter of languifhing patients; one of thofe ill bodeing creatures that haunt houfes againft a time of Death; a Devil that comes to torment men before their time. While the Divine prepares you for Death, and the Phyfitian haftens it, he does both. Like the Hangman, he firft difrobes you of your outer garments, and then kills you. That you may go to Heaven the lighter, he difburdens you of your Earth, your Eftate, and then perfwades you out of defpair to die, having parted with all the World, and nothing now left you to forfake, but your body. For a good Fee he will do a friend a Courtefie and leave the intended Heir fo difreputable, that the Deceafed Teftator may as foon interpret his own mind as the Lawyer : inferting fuch equivocal terms, as may be interpreted to be any mans Will more then the Teftators; rendring the fenfe as amphibious as that of the Oracles : and indeed like the laft words of dying man, ambiguous and unintelligible. If he foift in a good Legacy for himfelf, he knows 'tis paft difcovery; 'tis but fkipping it in the reading, and the Will fealed up till the Teftators Death, who can betray him? Thus he Cheats you In the Name of God, and fayes his prayers backwards indeed, beginning his Rogueries with an Amen : fo that you fign a blank though it be full of Writing, and this your moft Voluntary act is yet againft your Will. He begins very pioufly, and bequeaths your firft Legacy, your Soul, with a great deal of Complement to God Almighty; to whom he commands you with as much form of expreffion, and abundance of fignificant words, as if he made Indentures with the Almighty to receive you, and would be fure he fhould find no ftarting holes to evade the Articles. And he makes your Will like a Pharifees long prayer, with a houfe at the end of it. When he has done, he turns you over to the Divine, before whom he has commonly the honour to be preferred, and there he leaves you like a Chriftmas box, expecting no more out of you till you are broke. To conclude, like the Mullet, his blood is Ink; 'tis the skin of a Sheep, not the wooll that cloaths him. 'Tis one of the laft trades men can fly too, indeed the very laft, being but a more noble Thievery, a gentiler way of picking pockets : a ruined Perfons laft refuge, where he revenges his deftruction by repaying it : being himfelf undone, he ftrives to ruine other's; and like a right Devil, draws as many as he can into that hell where himfelf has perifhed. But I have made a Character as long as an Indenture; I leave him with the prayer of all good People, that he may be poyfon'd with his own Ink, ftab'd with his Penknife, his Ears remaine in the Pillory, his Nodle fet out at the Shop-door for a Loggerhead, and the reft of him hang'd up to Eternity in a Label; and fince it is impoffible he fhould get to Heaven, for Hell's fake may he hang between.

Finis.

Appendix III
WARDENS AND MASTERS

WARDENS

1392	Martin SEMAN and John COSSIER	1553	William BLACKWELL and William GARARD
1440	John GRENE and Robert BALE	1554	John MELSHAM and Stephen ALEXANDER
1446	John STODLEY and Thomas FRODDESHAM	1555	Richard MAUNSELL and Thomas PIERSON
1450	John GROVE and Robert BALE	1557	Thomas GODFRAYE and John STUBBERDE
1478	John MOREKOK and Henry WODECOK	1559	Thomas WENT and William PYRESON
1481	John PARKER and Thomas MASSE	1561	John NORDON and Bartholomew BROKYSBIE
1490	Henry WODECOK and Edmund TASBURGH	1562	Thomas WYTTON, sole warden after the death
1497	Henry WOODECOCK and		of John HULSON
1517	William CARKEKE and Richard STAVERTON	1564	Thomas PIERSON and Thomas ATKYNSON
1518	John WORSOP and John LEE	1565	William PEYRSONE and Stephen
1530	John DEVEREUX and John RUTTER		ALEXSANNDRE
1535	John REVE and William SWANE	1567	Thomas WYTTON and Anthony BONDE
1540	John STANNING and Christopher GRIGGS	1569	Thomas GODFREY and Peter BAKER
1541	John LEE and Edward BARBOURE	1573	Thomas WENT(E) and John DALTON
1543	John WORSOP and John LEE	1575	John NORDEN and Thomas BRENDE
1544	John RUTTER and William BLACKWALL	1576	John DALTON and Humfrey BROKE
1545	William BLACKWALL and William GARARD	1577	Peter BAKER and Anthony HIGGONS
1547	William SWANE and William CARKEKE	1580	Thomas BRENDE sen. and Frances KYDD
1551	Thomas WENT and William PIERSON	1583	Anthony HIGGONS and Paul POPE
1552	John MELSHAM and John HULSON		

From 13 September 1583, the names of the Masters of the Company appear and, with some considerable gaps prior to 1733, the list is continuous to the present day. Wardens usually went on to become Master, and those who did not are listed below in brackets and in italics.

MASTERS

1583	John DALTON	1618	John PARTRIDGE
1585	Paul POPE		Geoffrey PLACE
1587	Paul POPE	1619	Henry BEST	*(James COLBRON)*
1588	William SQUYER	*(William DERMER)*		*Clerk: John PLUKENETT or PLUCKNETT*
1589	George KEVALL	*(William SERCHE)*	1620	Robert MORGAN
1591	George KEVALL	*(Simon WRENCHE)*	1621	Francis KEMPE	*(William CHILDE)*
1593	William ONSLOWE	*(Robert PRESTON)*	1622	Peter BLORE (or BLOWER)
1594	John LANGHAM	*(William BROOKE)*	1623	Edward WHITE
1596	Bernard GARTER	*(Henry ALLISON)*	1624	Godfrey RAYNER	*(Humphrey PYE)*
1597	John TAYLOR	*(John CRAFFORD)*	1625	Charles BOSTOCK
1598	Thomas HULSON		1626	Richard WOOTTON
1599	Thomas CHAPMAN		1628	John WOODWARD	*(Jeffrey BOWER)*
1601	John COWPER	*(Bernard CASTLETON)*	1629	John WARREN	*(Robert WOODFORD)*
1603	William BENEDICK	*(Walter MEREDITH)*	1630	John MAYE	*(Richard ALIE)*
		(Edward PIERSON)	1631	Roland SQUIER
1606	George SAMWELL	*(John LAWE,*	1632	Francis MOSSE
		Walter FILKINS)	1633	Thomas HILL
1607	Thomas FITCH		1634	Charles YEOMANS	*(Stephen KING)*
1609	William BONNER	*(Thomas SMYTHE)*	1635	John MACRO	*(Edward CHAPMEN)*
1610	William BONNER	*(Robert BANCKWORTH)*	1636	Bartholomew GILMAN	*(John ATKINS)*
1611	Andrew TURNOR	*(John MAYLE)*	1637	John SMITHER
1613	Edward LEDSHAM	*(Robert HILL)*	1638	John SMITH	*(Robert MINCHARD)*
1615	William DODD	*(Robert GRIFFITH)*	1639	William AUDLEY	*(John RYE)*
1616	William DODD		1640	William ALEXANDER
			1641	Abraham CHURCH	*(George ALISTREE)*
			1641	John PRIDGEON	*(Matthew BILLING)*

1642	Thomas WANNERTON	1744	John Lewis BONNET
1643	Michael HOLEMAN	1745	William VAUGHAN *(Richard HUNT)*
1645	Thomas WANNERTON	1746	William HUSSEY
1646	Thomas WANNERTON	1747	George FARR
1647	Thomas WANNERTON (Part year)	1748	Edmund CHAUNTRELL
	Francis KEMP	1749	George JENNINGS
1648	Henry SHELBERY	1750	Josiah Bacon LONE
	Clerk: Christopher FAVEL or FAVELL	1751	Thomas WELCH
1649	James NOELL *(Francis WEBB)*	1752	Gideon GUICHENET
1650	Ralph HARTLEY *(John REA)*	1753	William MARTYN
1651	Humphrey SHALLCROSSE	1754	Robert WIGSTON
1652	Walter SMITH	1755	William BRADY *(Robert ROBERTS)*
1653	Nicholas BACON *(Martin DALLISON)*	1756	Edward ROBERTS
	Henry COLEBORNE	1757	William GINES
	Mark BRADLEY	1758	Robert WILLOCK
1654	Nicholas BACON	1759	George Woodward GROVE
	Humfrey HAYWARD	1760	Benjamin BONNET
1655	Thomas COLWELL	1761	Adam BARBER
1656	Richard SHELBERY	1762	William CAMPBELL
1657	Richard HOLEMAN	1763	James PRICE
	Clerk: William JEFFREYS (continuity unclear)	1764	William OSBOURN(E)
1658	John HALLIWELL *(Robert ABBOTT)*	1765	Richard RICHARDSON
1659	Martin NOELL	1766	William BROWN(E)
	Daniel WOOGATE	1767	William HOPKINS
1660	John ROBINSON	1768	Abraham OGIER
1661	Thomas BOSTOCK	1769	Benjamin VAUGHAN
1662	Edward PERRY	1770	Gyles LONE
1663	Joseph ALPORT	1771	Samuel VAUGHAN
1664	Henry MOSSE *(John SMITHER)*	1772	James JEFFERSON
1665	Richard ANDREWS (died)	1773	John ELLIS
	Henry OWEN	1773	Richard PAYNE
1666	Richard DUKE	1774	Robert SHANK
1667	John UNDERWOOD	1775	Benjamin VAUGHAN
1668	John ALSOP	1776	Edward CAHILL
1669	James WINDUS *(Arthur MILES)*	1777	Jeremiah BENTHAM
1670	John MORRIS	1778	William GINES
1671	Sir Robert CLAYTON	1779	Jeremiah HARGRAVES
1672	Solomon SEABRIGHT	1780	Joseph COOPER (Senior)
1673	Thomas COLWALL *(Thomas MASSAM)*	1781	William SEAGER (alias PARSONS)
1674	George PERRYER *(Hercules COMANDER)*	1782	John HICKS
1675	Joseph COOKE *(Leonard BOWER)*	1783	William Michel SALE *(Isaac COOPER)*
1676	Thomas GOODWIN *(William WARNE)*	1784	John ELLIS
1677	William BOWER *(William DAINES)*	1785	John MITCHELL
1678	Leonard BATES *(James NEEDLER)*	1786	Thomas CHAUNTRELL
1681	Clerk: William BRAXTON	1787	Silas PALMER
1702	Richard MANLOVE	1788	Benjamin Macy BURTON
1703	Richard MANLOVE	1789	Joseph WINDER
1712	Edward DAWGS	1790	Thomas HUBBERT
1716	*(Samuel DUNKLING)*	1791	Tobias ATKINSON
1717	*(Joseph RONDELET)*	1792	Thomas BONNET
1720	*(Ebenezer JONES)*	1793	John BROWN
1725	Jeremiah BENTHAM I		*Clerk: William Wheatley HUSSEY*
1731	*Clerk: Jeremiah BENTHAM I*	1794	Samuel GLAISTER
1732	Mudd FULLER	1795	John ALEXANDER
1733	Philip JENNINGS	1796	Reverend George NEAL
1734	William GWINNELL	1797	William GLAISTER
1735	Nathanial GIBBON	1798	Samuel BRADFORD
1736	John ELLIS	1799	Joshua OGIER
1737	John TUFF	1800	John STOKES
1738	John HUMPHRIES	1801	Joseph COOPER (Junior) *(John ATKINSON)*
1739	James RAVENS	1802	Robert ROBSON
1740	Robert DUNBAR	1803	Thomas STOKES
1741	James FLETCHER	1804	Robert Tomlinson MOORE
	Clerk: Jeremiah BENTHAM II	1805	Thomas LUMLEY
1742	Edward DAWGS		*Clerk: George NELSON*
1743	Gilbert POND	1806	James SHAW

1807	William DUFF
1808	John BEARD
1809	John IGGULDEN
1810	Archibald DUFF
1811	John VENN *(George ELLIOTT)*
1812	John WITHERS
1813	Tobias ATKINSON *(John TAVERNER)*
1814	Benjamin NEWTON
1815	John NEWTON
1816	Alexander LAMB
1817	John Hayward SPENCELEY
1818	John William NELSON
1819	George BRAINE
1820	Joshua OGIER
1821	Joseph COOPER (Junior)
1822	Robert Tomlinson MOORE
1823	John BEARD
1824	John VENN
1825	Thomas STOKES
1826	Benjamin NEWTON
1827	John NEWTON
1828	John VENN
	Clerk: Park NELSON
1829	George BRAINE
1830	John Robert SHERMAN *(Henry COOPER)*
1831	John Robert SHERMAN *(Isaac STRIDE)*
1832	Alexander LAMB
1833	George GUILLONNEAU
1834	William DUFF
1835	William SCORER
1836	Lewis STRIDE
1837	Edward CURETON
1838	John Wright SNOW
1839	William NICHOLS
1840	William à BECKETT
1841	John Sise VENN
1842	Charles Robert FORRESTER
1843	James COMERFORD
1844	John DONNISON
1845	Thomas Samuel GIRDLER
1846	John MATTHEY
1847	John MATTHEY
1848	James ANDERTON
1849	Timothy SURR
1850	John FIELD
1851	John HARRISON
1852	Frederick CLARKSON
1853	John PREEDY
1854	John NEWTON
1855	William Webb VENN
1856	Charles WINTER
1857	John MITCHELL
1858	James BENTLEY
1859	William GRAIN
1860	Alexander RIDGWAY
1861	Salem Constable HARRIS
1862	George Hooton DOWNES
1863	John Edward JOHNSON
1864	John Henry GRAIN
1865	Thomas Edward NEWTON
1866	William GRIBBLE
1867	Lewis CROMBIE
1868	James William COMERFORD
1869	Charles MATTHEY
1870	William Webb VENN
1871	James COMERFORD
1872	John VENN
1873	Richard MOSS
1874	George Thomason PEEVOR
1875	Charles Collier JONES
1876	John Cardy WOOTTON
	Clerk: William GRIBBLE
1877	Douglas John NEWTON
1878	Joseph Girdler WALKER
1879	William English HARRISON
1880	John Robinson ADAMS
1881	Francis JOURDAN
1882	Thomas Samuel GIRDLER *(John MERCER)*
1883	Edward Freston BUNTON
1884	Frederick William LAWRENCE
1885	Edwin FRESHFIELD
1886	Edwin FRESHFIELD
1887	John BRIDGES *(Alexander CROMBIE)*
1888	Wilmer Matthews HARRIS
1889	William GRAIN
1890	George HOLMAN
1891	William Eustace VENN
1892	Alan Charles COMERFORD
	Temporary Clerk: Walter Gouldsmith GRIBBLE
1893	George Holland MILFORD
	Clerk: John Cardy WOOTTON
1894	Robert Homfray James COMERFORD
1895	John Snow MOSS *(Frederick CHEESWRIGHT)*
1896	Henry Golding FREEMAN
1897	William GRAIN
1898	John Dalton VENN
1899	Henry WEATHERALL
1900	Horatio Arthur Erith de PINNA
1901	James William COMERFORD
1902	Edwin Hanson FRESHFIELD
1903	Charles Joseph WATTS
1904	John Alfred DONNISON
1905	John William Peter JAURALDE
1906	George Anthony KING
1907	Richard PHILLIPS
1908	Nicasio Robert JAURALDE *(John ATKINSON)*
1909	William CRAWLEY
	Clerk: Thomas John WOOTTON
1910	Frederick William LAWRENCE
1911	Edwin Courtney WALKER
1912	Henry Alfred WOODBRIDGE
1913	Joshua Dawson WATTS
1914	Russell Jourdan FREEMAN
1915	Edwin FRESHFIELD
1916	Alan Charles COMERFORD
1917	Robert Homfray James COMERFORD
1918	Harry Peter VENN
1919	John WATT
1920	John BROAD
1921	Arthur Elliot SHUTER
1922	James Dale WEATHERALL
1923	George Joseph Bayspool PORTER
1924	Noel Philip Wentworth BRADY
	Clerk: Arthur Alexander PITCAIRN
1925	John Dalton VENN
1926	Edwin Hanson FRESHFIELD
1927	Thomas John WOOTTON
1928	Edwin Courtney WALKER
1929	Joseph Phillips CRAWLEY
1930	John Edward NEWTON
1931	Henry Alfred WOODBRIDGE

1932	Joshua Dawson WATTS
1933	Anthony Highmore KING
1934	John VENN
1935	Kenneth Livingston STEWARD
1936	John Moxon BROAD
1937	Edgar Arthur BLOCKLEY
1938	Russell Jourdan FREEMAN
1939	Reginald Geoffrey BROAD
1940	Walter Frederick MURLY
1941	Felix William GRAIN
1942	George Joseph Bayspool PORTER
1943	Athro Charles KNIGHT
1944	Noel Philip Wentworth VYNER-BRADY
1945	Joseph Phillips CRAWLEY
1946	John NEWTON
1947	Anthony Highmore KING
1948	John VENN
1949	Kenneth Livingston STEWARD
1950	Wilfrid Maurice PHILLIPS
1951	Alan RICKETTS
1952	Philip Gage DWYER
1953	John Alfred CHAMBERLAIN
1954	Herbert Sutton SYRETT
1955	Patrick Francis Jourdan FREEMAN
1956	Gerald William HENDERSON
1957	Frederick Campbell GILES
	Clerk: Hugh Stuart Stucley TROTTER
1958	Sydney Charles CROWTHER-SMITH
1959	Edwin Bruce Courtney WALKER
	(James WILSON)
1960	Frederick WOOD
1961	David Ernest Thomas FLOYD EWIN
1962	John Alexander Robert CAMPBELL-MACKLIN
1963	Brian Guinness Clifford BROOKS
	(John NEWTON Jnr)
1964	Alan WALMSLEY
1965	Thomas Percy ROGERS
1966	Douglas Beresford Griffitt GABRIEL
1967	John LAZARUS-BARLOW

1968	Derek Wilfred JULIAN
1969	Anthony Jack BURGESS *(Arthur MORRIS)*
1970	Frank Dickinson LAWTON *(John PEDDER)*
1971	Joseph JENKINS
	Acting Clerk: *John Alexander Robert CAMPBELL-MACKLIN*
1972	Hugo Stuart Stucley TROTTER
1973	Adrian George ORCHARD *(Bryan ANSTEY)*
1974	John David WOODWARD
	Honorary Clerk: Desmond Victor O'MEARA
1975	Harold Mervyn TEMPLE-RICHARDS
1976	John Doughty HEAL
1977	Keith Francis Croft BAKER
1978	Alexander Colin COLE
1979	George Drewry SQUIBB *(Arthur OCKENDEN)*
1980	Leonard Charles HARMAN
1981	William Arthur Scotchings CAMP
	Clerk: Henry James William HARMAN
1982	John Francis PHILLIPS
1983	Robert Anthony Duff URQUHART
1984	Nicholas Ronald Rathbone SMITH
1985	John Philip Brooke BROOKE-LITTLE
1986	Martin John SCANNALL
1987	Robert Geoffrey SWAN
1988	Michael MACLAGAN
1989	Christopher John MALIM
1990	Ronald Stuart KINSEY OF KINSEY
1991	Gilbert Edward Isaac CLEMENTS
1992	Alan Howard COPE
1993	Bernard John DUCKER
1994	Albert Hamilton HAMILTON-HOPKINS
	Clerk: Peter Charles STEVENS
1995	Henry James William HARMAN
1996	Barry Desmond O'MEARA
1997	Donald JACKSON
1998	Oliver John Raymond KINSEY
	Clerk: George Andrew HILL
1999	Neil Alexander GRIMSTON

Appendix IV

CLERKS 1619-1999

'The Court is the Governing Body of a Company, and its chief executive officer is the Clerk. Clerks were first found to be a necessity during the sixteenth century …'. So wrote Sir Ernest Pooley, Clerk of the Drapers Company 1908-1944.[1]

The records of the Scriveners' Company show the following to have served as Clerk of the Company:

1. John Plukenett (or Plucknett) 1619-1648
2. Christopher Favel (or Favell) 1648-1658
3. William Jeffreys . . . . 1658 -1681
4. William Braxton 1681-1731
5. Jeremiah Bentham I 1731-1741
6. Jeremiah Bentham II 1741-1792
7. William Wheatley Hussey 1793-1805
8. George Nelson 1805-1828
9. Park Nelson 1828-1876
10. William Gribble 1876-1893
11. Walter Gouldsmith Gribble (temporary) 1892-1893
12. John Cardy Wootton 1893-1909
13. Thomas John Wootton 1909-1924
14. Arthur Alexander Pitcairn 1924-1957
15. Hugh (Hugo) Stuart Stucley Trotter 1957-1974
16. John Alexander Robert Campbell-Macklin (acting) . . 1972-1973
17. Desmond Victor O'Meara (Honorary) 1974-1982
18. Henry James William Harman 1982-1994
19. Peter Charles Stevens 1994-1998
20. George Andrew Hill 1998-

The first Clerk of the Scriveners' Company whose name can be traced in the records was John Plukenett or Plucknett, 'now Clerk to the Company', on 6 July 1619.[2] He was a Scrivener, like almost all his successors, and was himself admitted on 9 December 1596. He was son of David Plukenett of Bridport, Dorset, yeoman, deceased, and had been apprentice to Thomas Chapman.[3]

He was followed by Christopher Favel or Favell (1595 -1664) who is listed as Clerk in 1648 of St Andrew Undershaft, London, where he was a beadle. He was admitted to the Company on 3 July 1621, as son of Roger Favell of Barford, Beds., yeoman, and apprentice to James Goodyer.[4] Favell's name also appears in an Index of Scriveners in whose presence bonds produced in the Court of Requests were sealed and delivered, in 1623/4, and in the probate records listed in Appendix VI below.

The Company's office list of Clerks next shows William Jeffreys who became Clerk in 1658. No other record of him has been traced. Between Jeffreys and the next name in the Company's office list, Jeremiah Bentham, should come William Braxton, admitted to the Company in 1665 as apprentice to John Alsop.[6] The City of London Freedom Records, starting in 1681, contain numerous certificates of admission to the freedom of the City, endorsed upon the indentures of apprenticeship entered into seven years earlier, bearing the signature 'Willm Braxton Cler.Societat.' (i.e. Clerk to the Society-the term used in the Charter to describe the Company). Between 1681 and 1712/13 he either witnessed or endorsed at least 20 such documents.[7] Most of these indentures were written on parchment (or vellum) by the apprentices themselves, being Scriveners. Some were very finely written, including that of Lidia Callendrine, daughter of Louis and Rachel Callendrine, made free of the City in January 1698/9, endorsed 'Willm Braxton Clerk to the Company/Benj.Edmonds his servt.'.[8] The Callendrines were probably of Huguenot extraction, as were other 18th century Scriveners such as Adam Barbar, made free of the City in June 1752 by patrimony as son of Lewis (Louis) Barbar and presented by Gideon Guichenet, Warden.[9] In April 1697 Braxton endorsed the completed indenture of Samuel Hilden[10] in the fuller form 'Willmi. Braxton Cler. Societat. Scriptor.Lond.'

Braxton also endorsed the apprenticeship indenture of Jeremiah Bentham, himself subsequently Clerk (see below), and grandfather of the Utilitarian philosopher Jeremy Bentham (1748-1832). The indenture,[11] in Latin, described Jeremiah as son of Bryand Bentham Junr., 'Civis et Pannitonsor', Citizen and Cloth Shearman (despite the amalgamation of the Shearmen's Company into the Clothworkers in 1528); in the *Dictionary of National Biography* Jeremy's great-grandfather is described as 'a prosperous pawnbroker in the City of London, (where) his grandfather and father practised as attorneys'. The first Jeremiah was made free of the City in November 1705.

While other Companies' apprentices had from at least the 1670s been indentured using pre-printed proforma deeds, the first such indenture for a Scrivener found is that of William Inman, made free in Jan 1712/13.[12] To mark this modernity, Braxton endorses this, apparently his last freedom certificate, 'Willm. Braxton Clerke to ye Compy'.

The freedoms of the City enrolled during Braxton's Clerkship are interrupted by two Scriveners' indentures endorsed with other names as Clerk. That of Charles Barton[13] is endorsed 'Benja. Raye Clerk.Societat.' in August 1689; that of John Browne in January 1698/9 bears 'Wm. Lupton Cler. Com. p'dict.'.[14] No further information about Raye or Lupton has so far been traced and it must be doubtful if their inclusion in a list of Clerks of the Company can be justified.

From 1713 onwards Scriveners' City freedoms were mostly by redemption until 1728 and no document among those sampled (all Scriveners' documents from 1681 to 1714 have been examined) bears the name of the Clerk until 1748.

Endorsements include Sam. Dunkling, Guard. (Warden), December 1716; Joseph Rondelet, Warden, March 1717/18 (a Frenchman naturalised in 1687); Ebenezer Jones, Guard., September 1720; Jere. Bentham, Warden, 1722/3; Jere. Bentham, Master, November 1725, and again in February 1725.

In January 1735 Jeremiah Bentham, son of Jeremiah Bentham, scrivener, both of Aldgate, was admitted to the freedom of the City by patrimony. The pre-printed document, on which the actual date has been left blank, bears the note 'father's Freedom in Book C 28 Nov. 1705' (see above). He (Jeremiah Junior) was presented by W. Gwinell, Warden, and the witness was Thos. Tussingham, Scrivener.[15]

The first pre-printed apprenticeship indenture to include the Scriveners' Company's Arms on a shield placed within the curve of the stem of the initial letter 'T' found among the freedom records sampled is that of John Bayley, made free in September 1738.[16] It was witnessed 'Jere. Bentham' followed by a paraph which may represent the letters 'CS' (Clericus Societatis?).

The next unequivocal statement of a Clerk of the Company is Jeremiah Bentham, in September 1745, when the signature of 'Jere. Bentham, Clerk' appears on the indenture of William Brady, son of the Rev. Nicholas Brady of Tooting in the County of Surrey, Clerk, apprentice to John Humphries, Scrivener.[17] The same signature appears again in June 1748 on Henry Barker's indenture,[18] and must be that of 'Jeremiah Bentham Gent.', who at some time before 6 May 1752 made the English translation of the Company's Charter still in use. He also signed the indentures of Joseph Buckmaster and Benjamin Macy Burton, both made free in July 1753, as 'Jerh. Bentham Clerk'. When Robert Seager was admitted to the freedom of the City in April 1793, the indenture was endorsed 'Presented by Wm. Wheatley Hussey/Clerk/to ye Scriveners/Chamberlain of London/Inrolled 15th June 1759'. This is an illustration of the length of time a Scrivener might delay taking up his Livery.[20]

William Wheatley Hussey witnessed the indenture of Thomas Stokes, made free of the City in May 1796,[21] as 'Wm. Wheatley Hussey'. He did not sign the freedom Certificate from 'An Especial Court held on Monday the 17th day of September 1798', when James Shaw, 'Son of John Shaw, of Kilmarnock, in the County of Air (sic: i.e. Ayr), North Britain, Merchant', was made free of the City by redemption. This was the Scriveners' Company's second Lord Mayor, in 1805, who had a memorable dispute with the Prince Regent over his precedence in the City of London in which King George III supported Shaw against his own son. Hussey did however sign the document for another Scot, George Scougall, son of George Scougall of Leith, Scotland, Merchant, made free of the City by redemption in November 1804.[22]

The final document examined in the City Freedom Records, the indenture of 'Christopher Stoakes son of Peter Stoakes late of Bexley in the County of Kent, Master Mariner, deceased',[23] both provides a link with the Scriveners' Company's present hosts, then unincorporated, the Honourable Company of Master Mariners aboard HQS *Wellington*, and gives the name of the next Clerk, witnessed as it is by 'Geo. Nelson, Clk. to Mr. Hussey/Clerk of the Scriveners Company'. Stoakes became free of the City in May 1807, and George Nelson became Clerk of the Company in 1805.

The Clerk maintains a tradition of getting as much as possible out of two important little words when responding to the toast by the Master to the Clerk whenever the Livery dines together. After a lengthy recital of the titles of those present: 'Master, My Lord Mayor, Aldermen, Sheriffs, Masters, Wardens, fellow Clerks, fellow Scriveners, ladies and gentlemen …', he says, simply and clearly, 'thank you'.

Appendix V
SCRIVENER FREEMEN (1686-1725)
SCRIVENER ALDERMEN (1627-1831)

Details of those Freemen of sufficient importance to deserve biographical notices follow. For the majority, it can be stated that the Company is fortunate enough to have some lists surviving from the 17th century.

HENRY BEDELL was a freeman before 1686 and a liveryman between 1685-1700. He must have been born about 1663, and married Dorothy Percy, who was buried on 8 January 1693/4 at St Benet Fink and had issue and, secondly, married Sarah and had issue. He was a scrivener of Threadneedle Street and a governor of the charity school in Broad Street Ward. He died on 30 September 1728, and was buried on 8 October that year at St Benet Fink. His will is dated 17 August 1720 and proved on 8 October 1728 (PCC 280 BROOK- PROB 11/624,280) 1 (*Musgrave's Obituary*).

JEREMIAH BENTHAM was apprenticed to Humphrey Brent, a scrivener, on 1 November 1698. He received his freedom by redemption on 28 November 1705 and he was liveryman in or before 1732. He became free of the City on 28 November 1705 and was Master in 1725 and clerk between 1731 and 1741. He was the son of Bryan Bentham of the Minories, a pawnbroker and citizen and cloth-worker, by his wife, Anne Gregory. Jeremiah was born on 15 August 1683 and baptised on 26 August 1683 at St Botolph's, Aldgate. He was educated at the Merchant Tailors' School and married on 17 December 1706 at St Botolph's, Aldgate, to Rebecca Tabor of Headhill in Essex, and had issue. He was an attorney in the parish of St Botolph's, Aldgate, and a trustee of the charity schools at West Ham. He was admitted an attorney in the Court of Common Pleas on 13 November 1730 and died in November 1741. He was buried in Great Baddow in Essex and his will is dated 3 November 1741 and proved on 23 November that year (PCC 296 SPURWAY - PROB 11/713,296). He was the grandfather of the celebrated economist and writer on jurisprudence, of the same name, who founded University College, London.

HUMPHREY BRENT was apprenticed to Andrew Haynes on 4 February 1685/6 and became a freeman about 1694. He was free of the City in April that year, the son of the Rev. James Brent, vicar of Ashton Keynes in Wiltshire. He married, on 25 November 1701 at St Michael Greenhithe, Elizabeth Davis, who was buried on 4 January 1738/9 at Holy Trinity Minories and had issue. He was a scrivener of the parish of Holy Trinity Minories and was buried there on 27 September 1731. His will is dated 19 February 1730/1 and proved on 6 October 1731 (PCC 246 ISHAM — PROB 11/647,246).

JOHN CURRYER, apprentice to Henry Bedell, scrivener, 3 February 1696, freeman 14 June 1707, liveryman and in the court in or before 1732, freeman of the City May 1708, son of William Curryer of the parish of St Benet Fink, merchant tailor, and Margaret, his wife, baptised 4 July 1681 at Christ Church, Newgate Street, educated at Merchant Tailors' School, married 24 May 1707 at St Michael's Greenhithe, Mary Hancock, and had issue. He was a scrivener in Broad Street.

ROBERT STAMPER, freeman in or before 1682, liveryman in the court in or before 1702, born about 1655/6, married 1684/5 at St Mary Savoy, Rebecca Marshall, buried at St Benet Fink on 4 September 1694, and had issue.

LOUIS THOMAS, admitted a freeman having been apprentice on 28 October 1718, he was a scrivener of the parish of St Benet Fink, died on 28 September 1729 and was buried there on the 6 October that year. His will is dated 22 September 1729 and proved 7 October 1729 (PCC 281 ABBOTT -PROB 11/632,281).

WILLIAM STANLAKE, apprentice to William Waine, scrivener, 28 July 1681, freeman by servitude on 25 February 1689/90, liveryman and in the court before 1732, freeman of the City by servitude, February 1689/90, son of Richard Stanlake, city of Westminster, gentleman of the Inner Temple, attorney, admitted an attorney of the King's Bench on 13 November 1730. His will is dated 7 September 1745 and proved on 16 September 1745 (PCC 259 SEYMER -PROB 11/742,259).

WILLIAM WAINE, freeman in or before 1681, a working scrivener.

Scriveners' Company: List of Freemen

ALLPORT, Joseph, son of Joseph ALLPORT (born 8.7.1635). Made free by patrimony 27/4/1702.

ASHTON, Richard, made free by redemption February 1725/26.

BALLAND, Daniel son of Thomas BALLAND of London apprenticed to Jacob Peters 19.8.1680. Made free (s) ² April 1689.

BARTON, Charles, son of John BARTON apprenticed to Isabella SIMPSON 1.1.1680. Made free (s) October 1681.

BECKLEY, Thomas, free by redemption, December 1716.

BENTHAM, Jeremiah, son of Brian BENTHAM citizen and baker of London, apprenticed to Humphery BRENT 19/11/?? (year missing on document). Made free (s) November 1703.

BLAKE, Joseph, a Goldsmith by servitude made free of Company, redemption on petition of Mr. Chamberlain of the City of London for the sum of £2 6s. 8d. December 1692.

BOOVER, Perkins made free (s) June 1728.

BRADY or BRADEY, Richard, translated from Gold and Silver Wyre Drawers. Made free of Company February 1694 (document badly written on a scrap of paper).

BRENT, Humphrey, of Ashton Keynes apprenticed to Andrew Haynes 4.2.1685. Made free April 1694.

BROOKER, Simon, son of Richard BROOKER late of the parish of St Saviour Southwark, apprenticed to Phillip LUGGAR 19.1.1676. Made free (s) September 1707.

BROWNE, John, son of William BROWNE Citizen and Cordwainer apprenticed to John Alsop 23.10.1676. Made free by patrimony January 1699.

BRYANT, George, son of Anthony BRYANT, apprenticed to Thomas CARR 25.3.1695. Made free (s) February 1703.

CALANDRINE, Rachel daughter of Louis (Lewis) CALANDRINE of Greenstead in Essex apprenticed to Elizabeth BILLINGSTRY 1.10.1674. Made free October 1681.

CALLENDRINE, Lidia, daughter of Lewis CALLENDRINE of Mile End in the parish of Stepney apprenticed to Rachel CALLENDRINE 14.2.1688. Made free January 1699.

CARDEN, Samuel, son of Stephen CARDEN. Made free July 1692. Document badly damaged.

CARPENDER, William, probably son of Thomas CARPENDER of Farringdon Ward Citizen and Scrivener (died 1657). Made free of Company by patrimony 22.5.1696.

CARR, Bedford, son of Robert CARR of Chillington in Sussex apprenticed to Thomas CARR 17.9.1683. Made free October 1690.

CARR, Charles son of Robert CARR of Chillington in Sussex apprenticed to Thomas CARR 17.2.1684. Made free (s) January 1693.

CHILCOTT, Silvester, Citizen and Merchant Taylor. Made free of Company by patrimony 13.1.1701.

CLARKE, Thomas, made free of Company by redemption for the sum of £2.6.8. 24.5.1709.

COOLEY, Charles, son of Anthony COOLEY of Dublin apprenticed to John HUGHES 15.7.1682. Made free October 1690.

CRIPPS, Jacob, son of Thomas CRIPPS of Hastings in the county of Sussex, Mercer, apprenticed to Joseph BLAKE 16.5.1704. Made free (s) August 1711.

CURRYER, John, son of William CURRYER citizen of London, apprenticed to Henry BEDELL 3.2.1696. Made free May 1708.

DANN, John, son of John DANN apprenticed to Leonard BATES 3.5.1681. Made free January 1690 (in poll 1700-1722) n.g.1710.

DANYARDS, William, free by patrimony April 1690.

DAYNES, William (document being restored).

DREW, William, by patrimony an apothecary of London. Desirous of joining the Company by reason of divers friends in the Company. Made free upon the report of Sir Robert BEACHCROFT and Sir Samuel STANIER, alderman, upon payment of £2.6.8. Made free (r.on pet.) 1709 in poll 1716.

DUNKLYN, Samuel, apprenticed to John BARNE in 1676 for seven years. On affidavit of John BARNE's widow, that apprenticeship had been served dated 30.10.1707. Made free November 1707.

ENDERLEY, Ezekial, son of James ENDERLY of Staynes in Middlesex apprenticed to Nathaniel ENDERLY 25.7.1677. Made free December (1693 in poll 1700); n.g.1710.

FINCH, Charles, son of William FINCH of Southill in Bedfordshire apprenticed to Rowland SIMPSON 14.6.1674. Made free October 1681.

FINEY, Richard, made free of Company on recommendation of Mr. Chamberlain of the City of London in Mayoralty of Sir Thomas STAMP on 28.3.1693 for the sum of £2.6.8 by redemption.

FLETCHER, Richard, made free (s) July 1726.

FOX, George, son of George FOX citizen of London, apprenticed to Henry BEDELL 10.5.1705. Made free 1713.

FULLER, Edward, son of William FULLER apprenticed to ??? (document badly damaged). Made free (s) August 1689.

GERRARD, Maximillian, made free of Company upon petition of Mr. Remembrancer upon payment of £2.6.8. 29.2.1712.

GLANVILLE, Samuel, made free by redemption January 1724.

GREENE, Edward, son of John GREENE apprenticed to William JOYNER 3.10.1678. Made free April 1689 (in polls of 1700 and 1710).

GREENE, Francis, son of James GREENE of Fulmodeston-cum-Croxton in Norfolk apprenticed to Rowland SIMPSON 7.8.1678. Made free October 1689 (in poll 1700) n.g. 1710.

GREENE, Jonathan, son of Elizabeth GREENE apprenticed to Edmund MANTLE 20.7.1684. Made free (s) August 1695.

HARRINGTON, Joseph, son of Thomas HARRINGTON of Bewdley in Worcestershire apprenticed to Richard Brady 14.7.1681. Made free (s) August 1690.

HARRISON, Samuel, made free of Company upon petition of Mr. Remembrancer (being the last of four granted by the Court of Aldermen) upon payment of £2.6.8. redemption. Made free 24.3.1704.

HILDON, Samuel, son of Cornelius HILDON late Citizen and Salter apprenticed to John WING 29.9.1687. Made free by patrimony 19.4.1697.

HOOKER, John, son of John HOOKER of Grays Inn in Middlesex apprenticed to John WILLIAMS 22.7.1677. Made free April 1692 (in polls 1700 and 1710).

INMAN, William, son of Charles INMAN late of Kirby Malzeard, apprenticed to Matthew BROWNE 8.4.1703. Made free January 1713.

JERRARD, William, made free by redemption July 1720.

JORDON, William, made free by redemption November 1714 (in 1722, 1724 polls).

KEY, William, made free by redemption (in 1722, 1724 polls).

KNIGHT, John, son of John Knight Citizen and Scrivener apprenticed to Henry BEDELL. (Document badly damaged.) Made free April 1693.

KNOWLES, Edward, son of Edward KNOWLES Citizen and Lorriner apprenticed to Basil COTTERELL 21.3.1675. Made free (s) October 1698.

LEES, John, made free of Company upon petition of Mr. Remembrancer upon payment of £2.0.8. redemption. Made free 23.3.1704.

LLOYD, John, son of John LLOYD Citizen and Scrivener of London, who was made free on 21.7.1676. Made free by patrimony September 1708.

LLOYD, John, son of Morris LLOYD of Bucknell in Salop apprenticed to William BOWDEN 14.7.1679. Made free August 1689.

LLOYD, Thomas, made free by redemption September 1716 (in 1724, 1727 (of St Andrew Wardrobe) polls).

MARRIOTT, John, son of Thomas MARRIOTT of Canfield in Essex apprenticed to William BRAMPTON 3.3.1689. Made free (s) April 1697.

MASTER, Simon, son of Martin MASTER Citizen and Joyner apprenticed to William BARTON 21.2.1688. Made free (s) October 1698.

MEARS, Enock, made free by redemption January 1715/16 (in 1724 poll).

MITCHELL, Benjamin Brend, son of Stephen MITCHELL of Ratcliffe in Middlesex apprenticed to Daniel SHYLING 24.3.1690. Made free (s) August 1697.

MOORE, Samuel, made free of Company on recommendation of Mr. Chamberlain of the City of London on 3.8.1691 for the sum of £2.6.8d. redemption.

MORELLE, John, son of Caesar MORELLE of London, apprenticed to Ebenezer JONES 29.3.1704. Made free September 1711.

OSLAND, Thomas, made free by redemption July 1716.

PARSONS, William, son of Thomas PARSONS of Papworth in Cambridgeshire apprenticed to Robert RICHARDSON 30.11.1682. Made free (s) April 1692 (in poll 1700) n.g. 1710.

PEPYS, Robert, made free (s) February 1713/14.

PETERSON, James, made free of Company upon petition of Mr. Chamberlain (being the third and last granted by the Court of Aldermen) upon payment of £2.6.8. Made free 24.11.1710.

POPE, Ralph, made free of Company upon petition of Mr. Keeper of the Guildhall (being the third and last granted by the Court of Aldermen) upon payment of £2.6.8. redemption. Made free 20.2.1713.

RECKLIS, Thomas, son of John RECKLIS yeoman of Chillwill in Nottinghamshire apprenticed to John KNIGHT 12.7.1695. Made free (s) April 1703.

REELY, John, free by servitude January 1682.

REILLY, John, son of John REILLY of Lambeth in Surrey apprenticed to John ALSOP 27.10.1674. Made free January 1681.

ROUS, John, son of Jeremiah ROUS Citizen and Grocer of London, apprenticed to John WINTER 8.8.1690. Made free (s) September 1704.

RUSSELL, Jacob, apprenticed to Robert SMITH. Served six years of apprenticeship before Robert SMITH died. As son of Robert SMITH not free of City Jacob was made free of the Company upon payment of £5.0.0. redemption to Mr. Chamberlain of the City of London 2.3.1694.

SIMPSON, John, son of John SIMPSON of Poulton in Coniston Lancaster apprenticed to Ebenezer JONES. Made free August 1691; in (poll of 1700) n.g. 1710.

SIMPSON, John, son of Thomas SIMPSON Citizen and Joyner apprenticed to Robert ROGERS. Made free September 1691.

SKEVINGTON, Samuel, made free by redemption February 1725/6.

SKINNER, Samuel, Citizen and Draper of London by patrimony. Made free of Company by report of Sir William STEWART and Sir Samuel STANIER, aldermen, upon payment of £2.6.8. Made free 29.5.1713.

SPEIDELL, Francis, son of Curtis SPEIDELL of the Parish of St Mary Whitechapel. (Documents badly damaged.) Made free December 1692.

STANDISH, John, son of Richard STANDISH of Chelsea in the county of Middlesex, apprenticed to Sylvester CHILCOT junior 20.2.1705. Made free March 1713.

STANLAKE, William son of Richard STANLAKE late of the City of Westminster gentleman. Apprenticed to William WARUD or WARD 5.8.1681. Made free February 1690.

TAVERNER, John, son of John TAVERNER of London, apprenticed to Nathaniel ENDERBY 29.9.1693. Made free January 1701.

TEVENAN, Barnaby, son of Thomas TEVENAN of Dublin in Ireland, apprenticed to Thomas CARR 26.5.1703. Made free May 1711.

TRAVERS, Samuel, son of John TRAVERS Citizen and Scrivener of London, apprenticed to his father 26.7.1698. Made free January 1711.

VENNER, John, made free of Company on recommendation of Mr. Chamberlain of the City of London on 21.1.1696 for the sum of £2.6.8.

VERNON, John, son of John VERNON of Richmond in Surrey apprenticed to his father. Made free 21.12.1691.

WEBB, Needler, son of Henry WEBB apprenticed to James NEEDLER. (Documents almost destroyed by water damage.) Made free (s) August 1692 (in polls 1722, 1724 and of Old Change 1727).

WEBB, Thomas, son of Abraham WEBB tanner, of Kingston upon Thames in Surrey apprenticed to Gerard USHER 24.3.1684. Made free (s) May 1691 (in polls 1722, 1724).

WILSON, Abraham, made free by redemption December 1717.

WINTER, John, son of Anthony WINTER of Southwark in Surrey apprenticed to Jacob PETERS 1.3.1677. Made free August 1690.

WOOD, John, son of Simon WOOD of Kidderminster in Worcestershire, apprenticed to William PARSONS 24.7.1700. Made free 31.7.1707.

YATES, Thomas of the Parish of St Mary Matfellon at Whitechapel in Middlesex. Apprenticed to Thomas CARR 28.7.1687. Made free (s) August 1694. (Document damaged where father's christian name is recorded)

Scrivener Aldermen[1]

Date	Name	Ward	Vice
1627 Mar 8 (May 22)	Henry Best Scrivener (?) Died 1628; adm. October 1628	Queenhithe 1627	Rowe
1627 Apr 24 (and sworn)	Robert Morgan Scrivener 1627 Died 1627; Will (PCC 99 Skynner –PROB 11/152,99) cod. September 10; Proved October 30 1627	Billingsgate	Gardner
1641 Oct 17	Peter Blore Scrivener 1641	Castle Baynard	Hudson
1651 Aug 2	Michael Holman Scrivener	Walbrook 1651	Selvy
1651 Sep 2	Humphrey Shallcrosse Scrivener	Walbrook 1651	Smithsby
1653 Aug 30 (Nov 8)	John Peirce Scrivener	Farringdon Without 1653	Whonwood

1653 Nov 29 (Dec 6)	William Wilkinson Scrivener	Walbrook 1653 (elected Sheriff 1639)	Prince
1657 Dec 3	Martin Noell Scrivener Knighted September 2 1662; M.P. Stafford 1656-8, 1659; Wexford (Ireland) 1661-5; Court Assistants Levant Company 1658-9; Committee E.I.C. 1657-9. Died *c.* September 1665; Will (PCC 120 Hyde -PROB 11/318,120) September 23; Proved October 6 1665	Aldersgate 1657	Wainwright
1659 Oct 11	John Bentley Scrivener Died 1667; adm. June 26 1667	Farringdon Without 1659	Knight
1661 Jun 27 (and sworn)	Thomas Colwall Scrivener Died December, 1675; Will (PCC 146 Dycer -PROB 11/349,146 and 11/351,78) December 16; Proved December 22 1675	Broad Street 1661	Lewis
1663 Mar 5	John Smith	Bridge Without 1663	Wild
1664 Dec 1	Richard Skelbury Without 1664-6 (elected S. 1666) Died 1669; Will (PCC 37 Coke -PROB 11/329,37) January; Proved March 16 1669	Farringdon	Bilton
1668 Oct 6	Jonathan Blackwell Scrivener Sheriff Bristol 1652-3; Died 1676; Will (PCC 119 Bence -PROB 11/352,119) January 17 1673; Proved September 25 1676	Candlewick 1668	Albin
1669 May 25	John Morris Scrivener M.P. Bletchingley 1679; Died February 1682; Will (PCC 153 Cottle -PROB 11/371,158) cod. January 31; Proved March 28 1682	Cheap 1669	Colvill
1670 June 16[2]	Robert Clayton Scrivener translated to Drapers October 23 1679. Lord Mayor 1679-80	Cordwainer 1670-6 Cheap 1676-83, 1688, 1689-1707	Roberts Sheriff 1671-2

Knighted October 30 1671; M.P. London 1679-81, 1689-90, 1695-8, 1701-2, 1705-7; Bletchingley 1690-95, 1698-1701, 1702-5; elected for Castle Rising and Bletchingley 1705 (contested London 1690, 1702); Commissioner Customs 1689-97; Governor Irish Society 1692-1702; President Honourable Artillery Company 1690-1703; Colonel Orange Regiment 1680-1, 1689-90, 1694-1702; President St Thomas Hospital 1692-1707; Director Bank of England 1702-7; Master Drapers 1680-1. Died July 16 1707; Will (PCC 165 Poley), cod. July 11, Proved August 1 1707 (PROB 11/495).

SCRIVENER FREEMEN AND SCRIVENER ALDERMEN

1798 Sept 19[3]	James Shaw	Portsoken	Haxmett
	Scrivener	1798-1831	Sheriff 1803-4
			Lord Mayor

1805-6
Created Baronet September 1809; Chamberlain 1851-43; M.P. London 1806-18; President St Bartholomew's Hospital 1806-31; President Honourable Artillery Company 1829-43 (Treasurer 1810-18, Vice President 1818-29). Died October 22 1843.

1976	Alexander Colin Cole	Castle Baynard
	Basketmaker, Scrivener	1964-
	and Painter Stainer	

TD (1972), MVO (1977), CVO (1979), KCVO (1983), KCB (1992), Maj Inf Bn and Court of Assistants (1962-89) HAC (1963), Hon Bencher Inner Temple (1988) Fitzalan Pursuivant of Arms Extraordinary (1953), Portcullis Pursuivant of Arms (1957), Windsor Herald (1966). Garter Principal King of Arms (1978-92).

Appendix VI
Scriveners in Probate Records
(1658–1665)

In Volume I Francis Steer suggested probate records as a source of biographical detail. This has proved to be so in this sampling. The following names and particulars of scriveners have been extracted from Deposition Books of the Prerogative Court of Canterbury (1658-1665). The reference for these is PROB 24/1,2 AND 4-7 (the volume for 1660 is missing). In the references quoted below, the second number is the folio number on which the information appears. PROB 24 is the Class number for all the volumes. The great majority of the scriveners were deponents (witnesses) in cases in the Prerogative Court relating to disputed Wills. 'v' means verso-reverse side, and 'r' means recto-facing page.

ANLABY, Thomas 7/205 v
of All Hallows, Barking, London; aged 32 (July 1667). Wrote a will, and was a witness to it.

ALSOPE, John 2/143 v S/573 v 6/18 r
(1) of St Dionis Backchurch, London; aged 42 (1659).
(2) of same parish; aged 47 (1662); Citizen and Scrivener. Testified as to family affairs of Richard Alsopp, deceased; but the relationship, if any, is not stated.
(3) of same parish; aged 48 (Jan. 1665). Has practised there for 19 years and more. Gave evidence as to handwriting.

ANGELL, William 4/388 v
had a shop near London Bridge. (Mentioned by his apprentice, J. Rausse (see below).

ASKEW, JOHN 5/309 r
servant (apprentice) to John Eldridge for two years and more; born in St Botolph, Bishopsgate, London. Aged 16 (early 1663). Had witnessed a will.

AUSTINSON, Godfrey 2/271 v
of St Margaret, Westminster; aged 24 (1659). Drafted a will.

BAKER, Clement 4/181 r
A testator (died April 1662). Of London, gent., bachelor. Lived with John Wheatley, scrivener (see below), his partner, but died in a house at Lambeth, near the house of Mr. Tradescant, [the famous gardener]. Had a brother, Thomas.

BANKES, William 5/30 r
servant (apprentice) to Humphrey Satterthwaite, scrivener (see below) for over four years past; born in St Michael, London; aged 22 June 1664). Wrote a will at the testator's direction in January 1663, and was sent to take instructions for another will in May.

BANNER, Richard 6/309 v
of St Andrew Undershaft, London; has lived there 3 years; born in Birmingham, Warws.; aged 35 (June 1666). Was servant (apprentice) to Henry Lewes (see below). Witnessed a Will, July 1662.

BARBER, Thomas 6/401 r
of St Peter, Cornhill, London. Made a will in 1665, and took it to the testator at a house near Lower Quay, where he lay sick of the Sickness [the Plague of London]; read it to him, and witnessed his signature.

BARNARD, John 2/54 v
of St Albans, Herts., yeoman, aged 40 (1659). 'Getteth his living by teaching children to write, and by making bills and bonds and engrossing conveyances as a scrivener, and also by being a clerke to the Receavors of the Lord Protector's Revenue in the County of Lancaster'.

BASKERVILLE, Cornelius 5/405 r and 7/327 v
(1) 'domestic servant' (apprentice) to Edmund Williamson (scrivener) for 4 years past; born in St Sepulchre, Newgate, London; aged 19 (June 1664)
(2) servant to same for over 7 years, at Great St Helen's, London; aged 23 (Nov. 1667). Testified concerning two successive wills of one testator, and about his estate.

BATES, Leonard 6/161 v
of St Michael, Cornhill, London, Citizen and Scrivener; has lived there 27 years; aged 42 (March 1666). In July 1665 a testator sent instructions for his will, and came to Bates's shop later to ask if it was ready. He then desired Bates to go with him to the Bear Tavern in Cornhill, where the will was sealed and witnessed, by Bates and his then servant, David Middleton. The testator said that 'if any should see him in a scrivener's shop and shoulde informe his wife thereof, she would conclude that he hadd beene making or altering his Will'.

BECKWITH, William 4/21 v
of St Bride, Fleet Street, London; living there for 2 years or so. Born at Richmond, Yorks.; aged 41 (Feb. 1662). Drew up a will in 1657, and witnessed it. Testified that certain alterations had been made since the sealing of the will.

BILLINGHURST, John 6/78 v
of Staines, Midd.; has lived there over 16 years; aged 49 (1665). Drafted a will, to which he and his daughter Mary were witnesses. Mary, spinster aged 20 years, was born in the Isle of Wight.

BORNE, John 7/239 r
of Basingstoke, Hants.; has spent most of his life there; born at Kingsclere, Hants.; age not stated. Was sent for to an inn in Basingstoke to make a will, and was a witness to it, in Oct. 1664.

BOWCHER, John 6/321 v
of St Mary Abchurch, London; born in St Magnus near London Bridge; aged 33 (May 1666). Testified as to a bond signed by a testator, to which Bowcher and his servant Thomas Collins were witnesses in Dec. 1664.

BOWES, Stanislaus 7/72 v
of St Giles in the Fields, Midd., where he has lived over 11 years; aged 30 and more (April 1667); born at Medhurst (Midhurst), Sussex. On 21 Feb. 1667 was sent for to a house in St Clement Danes where he took instructions for a will; brought it next day and was a witness.

BRADSHAW, Henry 6/310 v
servant or clerk (?apprentice) to Henry Lewes, scrivener, for 5 years past; aged 21 (June 1666); born at Upsill (Upsall), Yorks. A caller came to his master's shop or study in order to have a will made, to which he (Bradshaw) was a witness.

BROWNE, Thomas 4/337 v
of the City of London; born at Walsingham, Norfolk; aged 26 (1662). Testified concerning mortgage transactions by a testator who had died in Dec. 1660.

BUNTING, Daniel 6/220 r
of St Christopher by the R. Exchange, London. Living March 1657; died before 1666. See CLEMENT, James.

BURDETT, John 4/349 r
of Maiden Lane, St John Zachary, City of London; has lived there 5 years; born in St Alphage, London; aged 40 (1662). Witnessed (at his shop) a will in Oct. 1660.
Also 471 r
of St John Zachary, Citizen and Scrivener, has lived there 7 years; aged 44 (1664). Drew up a will from instructions brought to him; and was sent for in March 1664 to prepare a codicil.

BUTLER, John 7/415
of St Catherine Creechurch, London; has lived there 15 years; born at Enfield, Midd.; aged 41 (Nov. 1667). The testator, whom he knew well, being sick of the plague, 'very much in London', sent for him in August 1665; Butler drew up a will from his instructions, but next day found him too ill to sign it.

CARWYTHAM, James 6/316 v
servant (apprentice) to Edmond Wynch, scrivener, for a year past; born in Stepney, Midd.; aged 17 (July 1666). Was a witness to a will on 7 Sept. 1665, in his master's shop.

CAUNDLER, Thomas 6/268 v

A deponent stated that in Oct. 1665 a testator of Waltham Abbey, Essex, sent for Caundler, 'a scrivener in the town', to make his will, but he would not come, not daring for fear of the contagion.

CLEMENT, James 6/220 r

of St Nicholas Acons, London, where he has lived 4 years and more; aged 26 (1665); born at Newton Morall, Yorks. Was servant or apprentice for several years to Daniel Bunting, late of the City of London, scrivener. Identified Bunting's signature, as witness to a will of March 1657, as being authentic.

COFFYN, Francis 5/550 r

of St Paul, Covent Garden, Midd., where he has lived 7 years; born at Mortimer, Berks.; aged 36(1663). In Nov. 1661 was taken to an old gentleman's lodging in the Strand to make a will for him; and witnessed it.

COLE, Charles 6/263 r

lodging near the Black Bull in Chicken Lane, in St Sepulchre, Newgate, London. Aged 23 or 24 (1666); born at Bishampton, Worcs. Is by profession a scrivener, and was apprentice to one Mr. Gregory, a scrivener, in St John Street, for 7 years and upwards. Left his service about 2 years since, was over 7 months at sea, otherwise in London. In Sept 1665 was in the shop of a scrivener, Mr. Simmons, in Long Lane, when Mr. Rich (an executor) came and asked him to go with him to make a will, which he wrote from verbal instructions by the testator. Was paid by Mr. Simmons 6/- out of 10/- he had received for the will. Later quarrelled with Simmons because Simmons offered him £500 to make the will void.

COLLINS, Thomas 6/321 v

?a scrivener's apprentice. Mentioned in a deposition by John Bowcher (see above) as his 'servant'.

COLSTON, Alexander, 2/50 r. See WILLIAMSON, William.

COPPING, George 7/76 r

of St Botolph without Aldersgate, London; has lived there since the Fire of London; aged 30 (April 1667). Was sent for to take instructions for a will, engrossed it, and was a witness.

CRESSENER, Robert 6/?

of St Bartholomew near the R. Exchange, London; notary public; has lived there about 3 months; aged 28; born at Bury St Edmunds, Suffolk. 'By profession a scrivener'. In May 1660 made a will for an old school-friend who had smallpox. Was a witness.

DALTON, Thomas 5/244

of St Olave, Southwark; has lived there 7 years; born at Brampton, Hunts.; aged 39 (Oct. 1663). Was sent for to make a will for a neighbour who had previously employed him to make some writings (deeds). Witnessed the will.

DAVIS, Alexander 6/338 v

scrivener, master of John How (see below). Deceased before May 1666.

DOMVILL, Nicholas 5/30 v

of St Clement Danes, London. Employed in making a will dated August 1662; and was a witness to it.

DRING, Simon 4/385 r

of St Botolph, Bishopsgate, London; born in St Augustine by St Paul's, London; aged 24 (1662). In 1655 was a servant (apprentice) to John Rolfe, scrivener, of Threadneedle Street (see below).

DUKE, Richard 5/481 r

of St Michael, Cornhill, London, for over 20 years; aged 47 (June 1664). Was sent for by a woman at Monken Hadley, Midd., to write her will, and was a witness.

ELDRIDGE, John 5/308 r

of King Street, Westminster, for 16 years past; born at Remenham, Berks.; aged 37 (Jan. 1664). In Jan. 1662 a man came to his shop and got him to make his will, which Eldridge and his apprentice John Askew (see above) witnessed.

FARNABY, Thomas 2/283 r

of Whitechapel, Midd.; aged 31 (July 1659); 'living and keeping a scrivener's shop at Wapping Dock'. Made and witnessed a will in Dec. 1657.

?FARON, Henry 5/107 r
of St Dunstan in the East, London; lived at the sign of the White Bear in Tower Street for 7 years past. Master of Thos. Quintyne (see below).

FAVELL, Christopher 5/78 v
of St Andrew Undershaft, London, for 40 years past; aged 69 (1664). Born at Barford Bridge, Beds. Drew up and witnessed a will. 'Had been usually employed by the testator in making leases and such affairs'. 'Hath been heretofore and is still Clerke of the Company of Scriveners, being bedle of the Ward where he lives'.

FELTHAM, Thomas 7/45 r
of St Ethelburgh, Bishopsgate, London; has lived there since the Fire of London, and previously in St Benet Fink parish for 9 months; aged 25 (Feb. 1667) born in the City of Norwich. In the time of the late visitation (Plague) was employed by the testator to make his will, a new one in Jan. 1667.

FOX, John 1/70 r
of St Bartholomew the Great, London; aged 49 (1658); keeps a shop in Duck Lane, Smithfield.

FULLER, John 2/114 r
of Jacobs Street, St Mary Magdalen, Bermondsey, Surrey; has kept a public scrivener's shop there for 7 years; aged 42 (1659). Wrote a will and witnessed it.

GARRETT, John 6/451 r
servant (apprentice) to Henry Minchard, scrivener, for a year and 5 months past; born in St Olave, Silver Street, London; aged 18 (Dec. 1666). Lives in St Saviour's Churchyard, Southwark. Testified concerning a will. See MINCHARD, Henry.

GILBERT, Thomas 2/30 r
of St Martin's Lane, St Martin in the Fields, Midd.; aged 30 (1659); 'keeping a publique scrivener's shop'. About 1 June 1658 was sent for to Long Acre to make a will, but found the testator unfit to give directions, through age and sickness.

GOODWIN, Thomas 4/48 r
of St Michael, Cornhill, London, for 22 years; Citizen and Scrivener; born at Parkehall, in Leigh, Staffs.; aged 37 (Jan. 1662). Was called to draft a will in May 1661; witnessed it.

GRIFFITH, Francis 2/218 r and 2/315 v
(1) of Christ Church, London; aged 32 (June 1659). Partner with his father-in-law John Hayne (see below). Both had been employed to draft a marriage settlement for a testator.
(2) of Newgate Market, London (in Christ Church parish); aged 30 (June 1659). Gave evidence concerning a will. Presumably these two are identical, despite the statements of age!

GROSVENOR, William 5/569 r
servant (apprentice) to John Houghton, of St Dunstan in the West, London, (see below) for the last five years and more; aged 20 (1664). Engrossed a Will by Mr. Houghton's direction, and was a witness to it and to a codicil in July 1664.

HANSON, Robert 2/238 r 1/158 r 2/77 v
(1) of St Mary Aldermary, London; aged 50 (Aug. 1659). His shop was in Bow Lane. Received instructions for preparing a new will, which his 'man' (assistant or apprentice) Richard Hawkins (see below) then drafted. Burnt the old will on testator's instructions.
(2) 'was employed by a testator as his scrivener and about several businesses for about ten years'.
(3) took instructions in 1654 for a will from a testator for whom he had done business for many years.

HARRIS, Henry 7/370 r
of St Clement Danes, Midd.; aged 60 (Nov. 1667). About Sept. 1665 was instructed by an old acquaintance to make a will for him, which he did, and was present when it was signed.

HATHORNE, Mr. 1/143 v
a scrivener in London, employed to write the will of Robert Baily, Esq., dated 6 Nov. 1657.

HAWKINS, Richard 2/321 r
servant to Mr. Robert Hanson (see above) of St Mary Aldermary, London; aged 26 (Aug. 1659).

HAYNE, John 2/216 r
has a country house at Islington, but works in Christ Church, London, and is a Common Councilman of Farringdon Ward Within; aged 53 (June 1659). Was employed to draft a marriage settlement.

HILL, William 1/216 v
of St Dunstan in the West, London; aged 42 (June 1658). 'Keepeth shop in Temple Lane, London'. Wrote a will.

HOUGHTON, John 2/117 v
of St Bartholomew, behind the Royal Exchange, London; aged 26 (Apr. 1659). Keeps a public scrivener's shop. Was sent for to Mark Lane to make a Will, and witnessed it. (Perhaps a son of John Houghton below.)

HOUGHTON, John 5/572 r
of St Dunstan in the West, London, gent.; has lived there many years; aged 50 (1664). Was employed by testator 'in several affairs of consequence such as by reason of his profession might need his aid and industry', including several successive wills. The last was 'reduced into writing and fairly engrossed' by William Grosvener (above).

HOW, John 6/338 v
of St Lawrence, Old Jewry, London; born there; aged 24 (May 1666). His master was Alexander Davis (see above), since deceased. Identified signature to a disputed will.

HOWELL, John 7/340 v
servant and apprentice to Thos. Walton (see below); born in St Botolph, Bishopsgate, London; aged 21 (Oct. 1667). Testified concerning will to which he was a witness in March 1666.

HOYLE, John 7/409 r
of St Giles, Cripplegate, London; born at Hopton, Yorks.; aged 24 (Nov. 1667). Visited a testator who lay sick; went to his own house in Billiter Lane and wrote the will; was present when it was signed. Was apprentice for 8 years to John Midgley (see below), 'but since the Fire hath had noe certaine dwelling place'-one year in Billiter Lane, now in Red Cross Street.

HOYLE, Samuel 4/349 v
formerly servant to John Burdett of Mayden Lane, St John Zachary, London; lived there 5 years; now in Gt. Wood Street; born at Almondbury, Yorks.; aged 22 (Oct. 1662). Took instructions for a will at Mr. Burdett's shop, and entered them in a book of instructions kept for such purpose; wrote the will and was a witness to it when the testator came in and executed it.

HUDSON, Nathaniel 1/20 r
of St Sepulchre, London; aged 34 (1657). In 1652, when living at the Little Old Bailey, drafted a will.

INGRAM, Robert 2/78 v
servant (apprentice) to Robert Hanson (see above); of St Mary Aldermary, London; aged 24 (Apr. 1659). Witnessed a Will.

KENNETT, Francis 6/187 r
of Stepney, Midd.; has lived there 17 years; born at Faversham, Kent; aged about 50 (1665). Was sent for in 1664 to make a will; wrote it, and was a witness.

KIFTELL, Philip 5/358 v
of St Sepulchre without Newgate, London. Citizen and Scrivener; there over ten years; aged 42 (Apr. 1664). In Nov. 1658 was called to a house in Ludgate to make a will, which he also witnessed.

KINGE, Mr. 1/66 r
'A scrivener in Soper Lane'.

KNIGHT, John 5/359 r
Citizen and Scrivener; formerly apprentice to Philip Kiftell (see above) whom he accompanied in 1658 to make and witness a will.

LANE, Thomas 6/295 r
of Snow Hill in St Sepulchre without Newgate, London; there about 7 years; born there; aged 20 (1666). Was sent for to make a will in Blackfriars, wrote it, read it aloud to the testator, and was a witness.

LEE, John 5/74v
servant (apprentice) to Robert Richardson, scrivener. Witnessed a will in May 1659.

LEWES, Henry 4/335 6/177 v 6/310 r
(1) of St Catherine Creechurch, London, gent.; has lived there 8 years; born in St Olave, Southwark; aged 36 (June 1663). Was called to a neighbour's house in 1659 to make a will for him.
(2) Drew up a will in March 1666, and was a witness.
(3) In 1662 witnessed a will, which he had himself engrossed. Aged 38 (June 1666).

LEWES, Humphrey 2/136 v 6/17 r
(1) of St Mildred, Bread Street, London; aged 56 (1659).
(2) of same parish; has lived there 33 years; aged 62 (Jan. 1665). Gave evidence as to the handwriting of a testator by whom he had been employed in several matters as a scrivener.

LIDGOULD, Nicholas 2/311 r 4/176 r
(1) of St Martin in the Fields, Midd.; born there; aged 43 (3 June 1659). Made a will, for a doctor.
(2) Drafted and witnessed a will in June 1660.

LOWTH, Mathew 5/401 v
servant (apprentice) to Edmund Williamson, scrivener (see below), in Oct. 1662, but died before June 1664.

MARRIOTT, Isaac 7/283 r
of St Sepulchre, Newgate, London, where he has lived over 3 years; aged 22 (Oct. 1667)

MARTIN, George 7/223 r
of Deptford, Kent; identified as the writer of, and a witness to, a will of 1663.

MASSAM, Thomas 4/122 r 6/99 v
(1) of St Bartholomew, next to R. Exchange, London, where he has lived about 2 years; born at Gisborough, Yorks.; aged 37 (Apr. 1662). In Sept. 1658 was sent for by a man who wanted him, or his partner George Perryer (see below), to write his will.
(2) Was a witness in Oct. 1662 to a will written by George Perryer.

MEDGATE, William 6/196 v
of St Giles without Cripplegate, London, Citizen & Merchant Taylor; has lived there 12 years; born at Dunstable, Beds.; aged 62 (Feb. 1666). Is a scrivener, and maintaineth himself and family by his profession. In 1665 a messenger came to his house or shop and dictated instructions for a Lady's will; he went to her house for her to execute it, but 'the nurse who attended on her came downe to them and told them that she was then dead, full of the markes and tokens of the plague'. (The Plague of London, 1665).

MIDDLETON, David 6/162 r
of St Bride, London; living there for two months; born in the parish aged 23 (1665). In July 1665, when servant (apprentice) to Leonard Bates (see above), witnessed a will.

MIDGLEY, John 7/410 r
of St Nicholas Olave, London (before the Fire). (See John Hoyle above)

MINCHARD, Henry 2/473 r 6/250 r
(1) of St Magnus, London; aged 25 (Dec. 1660). Brother of Robert, his partner (below).
(2) of St Saviour, Southwark, Surrey. Citizen and Scrivener; formerly of St Magnus the Martyr; aged 31 (Dec. 1666). In May 1666 a testator came to his shop in New Fish Street and gave instructions for a will, which he drafted and his servant John Garret engrossed, and he witnessed.

MINCHARD, Robert 2/473 r
brother and partner of Henry (above)

MINTERNE, John 6/522 v
of Limehouse, in Stepney, Midd., for 15 years past; aged 44 (1666). Made a will and witnessed it in Oct. 1666.

NICHOLSON, Andrew 4/278 r
of St Michael, Wood Street, London; there about 20 years; born in St Martin in the Fields, Midd.; aged 40 (1662). Drafted a will.

NORTON, Gravely 4/215 v 1/173 r
(1) of St Dunstan in the West, London, for 8 years; born at Barn Elms, Surrey; aged 24 (1662)
(2) one of the same name, 'counsellor at law and J.P. for Herts'; wrote a will, but not called a scrivener. ?father or near relative of the foregoing G. Norton (1658).

PAMAN, William 7/204 v
of St Andrew, Holborn, London; one and a half years there, and before one and a half years in St Bride's; aged 30 (June 1667); born in St Bride's. Was sent for to make a will at the time of the late Sickness, in Sept. 1665.

PARREY, John, 2/203 v
(1) of St Antholin, London; aged 37 (Sept. 1659)
(2) (spelt Parry) aged 40 (1662); has lived in St Antholin's the last 14 years; born there. Was sent for to make a will in May 1662, and witnessed it.

PAXTON, —, 4/210 r
of Barnabee Street, Southwark; Surrey. Mentioned as a scrivener.

PENNANT, Thomas 4/302 r
of St John the Baptist, London; born at Halkyn, Co. Flint; aged 67 (1662). Drafted a will in June 1662.

PERRYER, George 6/100 r 4/122 r
(1) of St Margaret, Lothbury, London. Citizen and Scrivener; there ?13 years and more; aged 25 (1665). Was sent for in Oct. 1662 to write a will, and witnessed it
(2) partner of Thomas Massam (see above) in 1658.

PETLEY, William 6/84 v
of St Mary Colechurch, London; there 3 years; born at Ightham, Kent; aged 30 in 1665. Drafted and witnessed a will in Nov. 1664.

PICKERING, Bartholomew 1/27 r 4/254 v 4/412 r
(1) of St John Zachary, Foster Lane, London; aged 35 (1657).
(2) same parish; there 14 years; born in Lombard Street, London; aged 40 (1662). Drafted and witnessed a will; had previously been often employed by testator.
(3) aged 42 (1663). Sir James Drax sent his coach to bring him to his house in Hackney to make a will; was a witness to it.

PLUKENETT, George, sen. 4/357 r
of St Margaret, Westminster; lived there 50 years; born at Wareham, Dorset; aged 66 (Dec. 1662). On Dame Catharine Vanlore's instructions dictated her will to his son (see below); was afterwards a witness to it. His house or shop was in New Palace Yard, Westminster.

PLUKENETT, George, jun. 4/356 r
of St Margaret, Westminster; born there and lived there the last 14 years. Aged 30 (1662). Son of George P., senior (above); lives with his father, who is of the same profession.

POPE, William 4/165 r
of New Sarum, Wilts.; has lived there 24 years; born at Caundle Marsh, Dorset; aged 47 (1662). Drafted and witnessed a will.

PORTER, Thomas 6/455 v
servant (apprentice) of John Minterne (see above) for about 3 years past; lives at Limehouse in Stepney, Midd.; aged 20 (1666); born at Orton on the Hill, Leics. In his master's absence, was sent for to take instructions for a will.

POWNSETT, Thomas 2/151 v
of St Lawrence Jewry, London; aged 37 (1659). Was sent for to make a will.

QUINTYNE, Thomas 5/107 r
domestic servant (apprentice) of Henry ?Faron (see above); born in the precinct of the Tower of London; aged 18 (1663). In his master's absence was called to a testator's house.

RAUSSE, Jeremiah 4/388 r
of St Olave, Southwark; there about a year; born at Harwich, Essex; aged 22 (Dec. 1662). Lived with his parents

in St Catherine by the Tower until he was apprenticed for nearly 8 years to William Angell. Was sent for in Sept. 1662 to make a will, and was a witness to it.

RAY, Sir John 6/130 v
'Mr Ray the scrivener, now Sir John Ray, at his house within Temple Bar' (mentioned in a deposition of 1666).

RICHARDSON, Robert 5/74 v
'a scrivener' (1663).

ROBINSON, John 5/518 r
of St Christopher, London. Perhaps a retired scrivener; left a bequest of £100 to the Scriveners' Company in his will, made 4 June 1664, after being taken ill while playing bowls at the Blue Bell in Edmonton.

ROCHDALE, Mr. 1/239 r
A scrivener, mentioned 1657.

ROLFE, John 4/385 r
of Threadneedle Street,London (1662); St Mary Woolnoth (1664); there half a year. Aged 50 (Nov. 1664). On instructions, caused a will to be drawn and engrossed, and was a witness to it in August 1664. Father of Edmund Rolfe, Citizen and Goldsmith.

ROSE, Robert 4/328 r
of Wapping, in Whitechapel, born at Ratcliffe in Stepney; aged 22 (July 1662). Made and witnessed a will in Dec. 1559.

RYTON, Thomas 1/27 v
servant & apprentice to Bartholomew Pickering (see above); aged 20 (1657).

SALISBURY, William 5/77 r
of All Hallows Minories, London. Drew up a will in Jan. 1663. See Sleigh, James.

SATTERTHWAITE, Humphrey 5/30 r 5/132 v
(1) of St Peter, Westcheap, London (mentioned in a deposition by his 'servant', Wm. Bankes).
(2) has lived in (the above) parish most of his life; born in St Michael, London; aged 35 (1664).

SAW, Samuel 6/276 r
of St Michael, Wood Street, London, Citizen and Scrivener; has lived there 3 months; aged 24 (1665 or 1666). In 1664 a testator called at his shop, then in Lothbury, gave him instructions for a will, which he 'did sett down in his booke which he kept for such purposes'; and returned later to execute the will, he (Saw) being a witness.

SHAW, John 5/328 v
of St Mary, Bermondsey, Surrey, where he has lived 8 years; born at Ayston in Macclesfield, Lancs. (Cheshire); aged 37 (Oct 1663). Was called to a testator's house to make his will, which he also witnessed.

SHAW, Jonathan 6/404 v
of St Andrew, Holborn, Midd.; has lived there over 20 years; aged 36 (June 1666). In Sept. 1665 testator came to his shop over against Gray's Inn Gate in Holborn. Shaw wrote a codicil for him, and witnessed it.

SHEPARD, Francis 2/417 v
of St Michael, Cornhill, London; aged 54 (Sept. 1659).

SIMMONS, Mr. See Cole, Charles (above).

SIMMONS, Mr. 5/77 r
Servant and apprentice of Wm. Salisbury (see above); born in St Michael Crooked Lane, London; aged 19 (May 1663). Was sent to a testatrix by his master, who had drawn up a will for her; Sleigh completed blanks left for legacies, and saw it sealed and witnessed.

SMITH, James 1/75 r
of Stepney, Midd.; aged 26.

SMYTHER, John 4/361 r
of St Faith the Virgin, London; born there and has lived there most of his life; aged 40 and upwards. 'Liveth on his estate and profession'. Was sent for in Nov. 1661 to complete a will, to which he was a witness the next day.

STANNARD, William 2/310 v
of St Botolph Aldersgate, London: aged 40 (June 1659). Drafted and transcribed Will and codicil.

SWINNERTON, Thomas 4/279 v
servant (clerk) to Andrew Nicholson (see above) in 1662.

TALBOTT, Mr.
'A scrivener', mentioned in 1657.

TAYLOR, James 6/451 v
of Houndsditch, in St Botolph Without Aldgate, London, notary public (but described himself in evidence as being by profession 'a scrivener'); aged 42 (1666). On instructions, he drafted and wrote a will, to which he was a witness.

TOTHILL, Stephen 6/85 v
of Cheshunt, Herts., where he has lived 21 years; born in St Giles, Cripplegate, London; aged 45 (1665). Was sent for and wrote a will from testator's instructions. Testified also concerning a nuncupative codicil.

TRAVERS, Henry 2/27 r 4/346 v
(1) of St Sepulchre Without Newgate, London; aged 51 (1659). Witnessed a will at Hammersmith, Oct. 1658.
(2) Born at Chipping Norton, Oxon.; aged 55 (Oct. 1662). Wrote and witnessed a will.

TRYM, John 1/268 v
now living at Wisbech, Cambs., gent.; aged 40 (Nov. 1658). Was employed by a testatrix in several businesses, wrote her will ('being a scrivener') in April 1655 and a codicil 4 months later.

WALLACE, James 6/184 r   6/305 r
(1) of Wapping, Midd.; has lived there 16 years; born at Dublin, Ireland; aged 30 (1666). Being sent for, found the testator lying sick; his will of May 1665 was produced and read aloud by Wallace, who then, on request, wrote an addition to it, which he witnessed.
(2) Was sent for, in 1662, to a house in Shadwell, where a testator struck out several legacies from a will and added others; Wallace then drafted a new will, and witnessed it.

WALTER, Lewis 7/223 r
of Deptford, Kent, where he has lived 34 years; born at Tiddenham, Glos.; aged 47 (July 1667). Identified handwritings of a testator, and of George Martin of Deptford, scrivener. 'Liveth on his profession and his estate, and is worth £100, his debts paid.'

WALTON, Thomas 7/302 v
of St Giles, Cripplegate, London. Citizen and scrivener; born at Marchington, Staffs.; aged 42 (Oct. 1667). Wrote a will on testatrix's instructions, and it was signed in his house in Bow Lane, in his presence. Brother of William (below).

WALTON, William 7/340 v
was given instructions by his brother to engross the will drafted by Thomas; and was a witness.

WARNE, William   4/390 v
of St Michael, Wood Street, London; there about 14 years; born at Ringwood,
Hants.; aged 36. Being sent for in Jan. 1662, made a will for the testatrix (for whom he had written a previous one). She asked after his wife and little boy. He was a witness.

WESTON, John 6/523 v
of the City of Westminster, for about 20 years; aged 39 (1666); born at Boddington, Northants.; In July 1666 wrote and witnessed a will.

WHEATLEY, John 4/129 r 4/182 v
(1) of St Margaret, Lothbury, London; there a year and more; born in All Hallows Staining, London. Was previously 10 years in Clerkenwell. Aged 55 (March 1662). Drafted a will, but by the time he came with his fair copy, the testator was too ill to sign.
(2) Born in Mark Lane, London. Partner of Clement Baker, the testator (see above) and lived in the same house. He and his son John were witnesses to Baker's will. Wheatley had a wife, Mary, married 17 years, and two children; the wife, also a deponent, said she was born at Aylesbury, Bucks. and aged 48.

WIDOSON, Philip 2/116 r 2/469 r
(1) of Shad Thomas, in St Olave, Southwark; aged 37 (Apr. 1659). Drafted and witnessed a codicil.
(2) born at Burton Joyce, Notts. Testified concerning a sealed will, which he opened.

WILLIAMS, Edward 2/473 r
servant (apprentice) to Robert Minchard (see above). Lived in the same house as Henry Minchard (St Magnus, London). Wrote a will which was signed in May 1660.

WILLIAMSON, Edmund 5/401 r 7/330 r
(1) of St Peter, Cornhill, London; there 16 years; born at Felsted, Essex; aged 44 (June 1664)., His shop was in Cornhill. Drew up a will in 1662, to which he was a witness; in May 1664 was sent for to Stepney, and made a new will.
(2) stated by his apprentice Cornelius Baskerville to have been employed by the testator in his affairs and business, such as making bonds and bills and other writings and conveyances …' and did usually consult with him in the disposing and putting forth of his moneys and in purchasing of lands and the drawing of deeds and evidences.

WILLIAMSON, William 2/50 r
of St Nicholas Olave, London; aged 21 (Feb 1659); servant (apprentice) to Alexander Colston, scrivener.

WINGE, John 7/131 v
of St Ethelburga, Bishopsgate, London; born in St Bride, Fleet Street; aged 26 (Apr. 1667). Witnessed a will in July 1658 and wrote another for the testatrix in 1665.

WOOLFE, Powell 2/205 r
stated to have drafted a will from dictation. Died before Sept. 1659.

WOOLSTON, John 4/460 v
of St Dunstan in the East, London; there 30 years; born in Coventry; aged 50 (Jan. 1663). Made a will in 1658, and altered it for the testator in 1662.

Notes on some additional Scriveners from Vol.6 of the witnesses' depositions in cases relating to disputed Wills etc. among the Probate Records of the Prerogative Court of Canterbury. (Public Records Office, PROB 24.)

VOLUME 24/6

BROMHED (a stray reference) 332 v.
The testatrix lodged in the house of Mr. Bromhed, a scrivener in St Martin's lane.

BUNTING, Daniel 220 (recto)
late of the parish of St Christopher's near the Royal Exchange, scrivener. According to his apprentice James Clements, witnessed a will in March 1656/7. Apparently since deceased (evidence given in March 1665/6).

CALVERLEY, Francis 312 (r & v)
by profession a scrivener. About 27 February 1665/6 was sent for to the house of Jane Page in St Giles in the Fields, to make her will, which he wrote, and to which he was a witness.

CLEMENT, James (same ref.)
of St Nicholas Acon, city of London, scrivener. Has lived there 4 years and more. Age 26, born at Newton Morrell, Yorks. Was apprenticed to (the late) Daniel Bunting; identified his signature.

COLE, Charles 263 v
now living near the Black Bull in Chicken Lane, St Sepulchre without Newgate, London. Aged about 23 or 24; born at Bishampton, Worcs. Is by profession a scrivener, and was apprentice to one Mr. Gregory, scrivener, in St John Street, for 7 years and upwards, and did exercise his profession in the shop of Mr. Simmons, a scrivener in Long Lane. Was not a Master Scrivener at the time in question, but was employed by Mr. Simonds [*sic*], but not as his menial servant nor for any wages. Was offered £500 to make the will in question void, but said he would not do so for £1,000.

COTES, Henry 462 v
a scrivener, wrote a will on 2 June 1664, and was a witness.

DIBBS, John 414 v 415 r
was sent for and made a will for a woman sick of the plague, on 24 October 1664. His master (not named) had lately died of the sickness. Dibbs himself is since also dead (1666).

HART, William 427 r & v
a scrivener, living in Mercer Street, St Martin-in-the-Fields, wrote and witnessed a will about the beginning of September 1665.

HOW, James 396 v
a scrivener, made a will for the testator, in a house in the Old Jewry, City of London.

MINTERNE, John 455 v
a scrivener, living at Limehouse in Stepney. Being engaged when a message was brought asking him to come and make a will, he sent his servant Thomas Porter (on 26 September, 1666). Porter (? an apprentice) took down, read aloud, and witnessed a will, on 22 September 1666.

RETHERECKE 405 r
a codicil was signed and witnessed in the shop of one Mr. Retherecke, scrivener, over against Gray's Inn Gate in Holborn.

TAYLOR, James 451 v
living at Houndsditch in St Botolph without Aldgate, notary public, aged 42, James Taylor. 'Being by scrivener' a will for which a messenger came to his house on behalf of a sick woman. Lived formerly (before the Fire of London) in Threadneedle Street.

Appendix VII
THE IRISH ESTATES[1]

The rebellion of the Earls of Tyrone and Tyrconnell led to the forfeiture of the county of Londonderry to the Crown in 1608. King James I clearly took a personal interest and, ever ready to gain peace while extending his profits, he was largely responsible for the development of the county. Several letters to the Lord Deputy in Ireland, Sir Arthur Chichester, written in the hand of the King himself, discuss the process of the King's scheme to 'plant' these lands with English or Scots, who would be trustworthy and loyal.[2] Irish tenants were also to be allowed if their record of loyalty was good. The Ulster Plantation was ultimately a somewhat brutal affair for the native Irish, and disturbing for the livery companies.

What might be termed a 'prospectus' was issued early in 1609. Applications were invited from people wishing to 'undertake' plots of land. Captains and officers who had served in those parts were specially recruited. English and Scots undertakers were to pay lower rents than Irish ones because of the obligation placed upon them to build castles and strong houses to defend the land against rebellion. Apart from a few of the nobility, only two people signed up. There had been too many strings attached, such as that which stipulated castles were to be built and manned within two years. That was an impossibility if native labour were not to be used.

So in May 1609 the King approached the City of London. He sought to compel the City Companies to support the Plantation of the City of Derry, the castle and town of Coleraine, and the twenty miles of country in between, the whole area being bounded by the River Bann to the east, the River Derry (or Lough Foyle) to the west, and the sea to the north.

King James wanted the Companies to provide money, not people, for the Plantation, and there was a great deal of negotiation. The City Corporation also sent Commissioners to Ireland, to assess the Plantation's commercial prospects, on the principle that if it could be presented as an excellent investment the Companies might join in more willingly. This worried the Privy Council sufficiently to write to the Lord Deputy in August that he should:

> ... select discreet persons to conduct and accompany them [the Commissioners], who shall be able to control whatever discouraging reports shall be made to them out of ignorance or malice. ... The conductors must take care to lead them by the best ways, and to lodge them in their travel, where they may if possible receive English entertainment in Englishmen's houses. ... Matters of distaste, [such] as fear of the Irish, of the soldiers, of cess [rebellion], and such like be not so much as named

The City's Commissioners became convinced of the prospects of the scheme, although an element of pure chance had been involved-for instance the Commissioners were impressed with one small town where, just as they arrived, the inhabitants were assembling to make their annual oath of allegiance to the Crown. The Lord Deputy wrote to the Privy Council in astonishment that the townspeople had assembled at all, compared with their conduct in earlier years. He also prayed God that the Commissioners 'prove not like their London women, who sometimes long today and loathe tomorrow'.

On 15 December 1609 the City Corporation decided to raise £15,000 for the Plantation from the Companies as a tax, 'according to the rate of corn set upon every company', i.e. each Company's obligation at that time to ensure that bread in the City was plentiful, so as to prevent shortages and rises in price. The Privy Council raised this figure to £20,000, because of the private interests which needed to be bought out, and on 28 January 1610 the City signed an agreement with the Privy Council to proceed with the Plantation on this basis.

On 30 January 1610 the Common Council also determined to form a body to manage the business, the 'Irish Society'. It received its Royal Charter on 29 March 1613. The preamble to this Charter contains some wonderful, not to say embarrassing, Jacobean English:

> ...Whereas there can be nothing more kingly than to establish the true religion of Christ among men hitherto depraved and almost lost in superstition; to strengthen, improve and cultivate by art and industry countries and lands uncultivated and almost desert, and the same not only to plant with honest citizens and inhabitants, but also to renovate and strengthen ... with good statutes and ordinances, whereby they may be more safely defended not only from the corruption of their morals, but from their intestine and domestic plots and conspiracies ... And whereas the province of Ulster ... for many years ... past hath grossly erred from the true religion of Christ we ... have esteemed it to be a work worthy of a Christian prince, and of our royal functions, to stir up and recall the same ... from superstition, rebellion, calamity and poverty ... to religion, obedience, strength and prosperity ... [etc] ... [3]

The City had some difficulty raising the £20,000, even by instalments, and the Wardens of the Mercers were actually imprisoned for a time by the Lord Mayor for non-compliance.

On 22 May 1611, King James instituted the Order of Baronets under a specious plea of their assisting him with raising money for the maintenance of troops in Ireland. Persons holding land worth £1,000 a year of good standing and bearing arms from the paternal grandfather were eligible to purchase the dignity for £1,095. As a further means of swelling the coffers, in 1616 eldest sons of baronets became entitled to claim knighthood on coming of age . [4]

The 'mere Irish', as they are referred to in the documents, fared badly. Although they had submitted themselves to the King's mercy, their legal status was almost entirely one of tenants at will of the rebellious Irish nobility. They were therefore summarily evicted by the planters. Not surprisingly, they were much upset and plotted rebellion, declaring that they would rather die than be removed to the small portions assigned to them. Many sought a new dwelling in other counties.

The Lord Deputy wrote to London in September 1613, 'The priests now preach little other doctrine to them but that they are a despised people, and worse dealt with than any nation that hath been heard or read of.'

Life was hard for the Companies too. By October 1615 they had contributed no less than £57,500, a fantastic sum. The Scriveners had paid £545; between 1613 and 1616, the total of five contributions to levies made by the Company of Writers of the Court Letter was £570. According to their petition for incorporation in 1616 they had levied £275 and had to find a further £73 required by the Worshipful Company of Ironmongers, with whom they had entered into a private plantation. The Company had no lands or stock and members refused to pay assessments or quarterage. [5]

The King wrote personally to the Lord Deputy in March 1615 expecting greater 'zeal and uprightness' in carrying out the good work, for progress was poor. The problem was that the undertakers were unwilling to evict the native Irish, partly perhaps because their labour was needed for construction, although the native Irish were not very willing workers. There was also a general inertia and, perhaps, also there were other pure humanitarian reasons.

A conspiracy in May 1615 to attack and destroy Derry and Coleraine was reported to the Privy Council. The Hallkeeper of Guildhall was instructed to forward arms and ammunition, assembled by the Great Twelve companies, to Ireland for its suppression. As late as the summer of 1624 the Privy Council needed to make up the troops in Ireland to 400 horse and 3,600 foot. This was more than double what it had been before.

In April 1618, the administration of the Plantation took a new turn. After long negotiations with the Companies and the Privy Council, the Irish Society divided up the county of Londonderry amongst the Great Twelve Companies. The lands were allotted to each of them by drawing lots, and the minor companies were associated with the Great Twelve again by lot. Each group of companies was compelled to purchase lands for a further £5,000. The towns of Derry and Coleraine and the fisheries and ferries were reserved to be administered directly by the Irish Society.

It is not immediately clear whether this had always been intended, or was yet another means of squeezing help out of the Companies. It is also unclear whether the Companies were required to 'plant' their new freeholds with Protestants, whether the Irish Society was to provide suitable tenants, or whether the existing populations were now more acceptable than before.

The Scriveners ended up in a group headed by the Ironmongers, along with the Brewers, Coopers, Barbers and Carpenters. The estate was formed into a 'Manor', the Manor of Lizard, named after the lizard supporters of the Ironmongers' Company's coat of arms. We know from the Ironmongers' archives that the earliest Scriveners' representatives to the managing committee were Mr. Griffin, Mr. White and Mr. John Woodward, and that Mr. Francis Kemp and Mr. White, again from the Scriveners, were the auditors.

As the Clerk of the Scriveners put it to the Livery Companies Commission in 1881:

> The Ironmongers Company are the owners of the Manor of Lizard in the County of Londonderry which they acquired in 1618 for £5000, the whole of which they did not pay out of their own moneys. The balance was contributed by several smaller companies, the Scriveners' Company contributing £570 which sum was obtained by compulsion from the private resources of the various members of the company, amongst them John Milton the father of the poet. He and the other contributors passed a resolution subsequently that the Contributions referred to in the resolution should thereafter belong to the Company and not to themselves. Hence the profession of the share in the Ironmongers' estate.

The Clerk added that the estate produced little income until the long lease fell in around 1843–less than £100. In the 1870s the Company's proportion of the rents produced an income of between £300 and £500 p.a. [6]

It appears that up to 1843 the estate was held on a long lease by a 'middleman', i.e. the entire estate was farmed out for a fixed fee, the lessee making his profit from whatever extra he could squeeze out of the actual occupiers. It was also held as one block, not subdivided by company, and administered by the Ironmongers for the group of Companies who were joint owners. If the Ironmongers' involvement was indirect, though, the Scriveners' was even more so. The Ironmongers' archives do include a report of a visit of inspection in September 1823 by Mr. William Parnell, commissioned by the Ironmongers to find out both what was going on and 'the best means to be adopted for the improvement of the tenants' situation at the expiration of the present lease'.

Parnell found the general state of the tenantry to be very poor, and fulminated against the 'middleman' system. An Ironmongers' representative visiting in 1830 was actually petitioned by the tenantry that the Companies should take their estates in hand and manage them directly. The Ironmongers' Company seems gradually to have accepted this argument, for in 1843 it assumed direct control of the Irish estates. In so doing it increased the income to the Companies substantially.

Greater involvement also led to greater record-keeping, and from then on the Ironmongers' archives include letters sent and received, committee minutes, rentals, and also inspection reports at intervals of every three or four years. Although such records inevitably present the activities of the Company in a good light, it still seems clear that the companies were fair and business-like landlords, concerned to create contented and prosperous tenancies, and not to oppress the poor.

The Committee which managed the estates consisted of representatives of the various Companies in the Ironmongers' group, including John Donnison from the Scriveners. In the early 1840s the Committee was frequently concerned with charitable grants, providing (for example) seed potatoes for the poorer tenants, and £10 for prizes for the best turnips at a local show. At one single meeting, in July 1846, grants were awarded to: The Agricultural Society of Ireland … £10; The new school at Garvagh … £10; The Presbyterian minister at Crossgar … £5; Building a meeting house at Garvagh … £5; Garvagh Scientific Institution … £2 2s, plus an annual £1 1s. towards the Schoolmaster's library there.

Curiously, there do not appear to have been any Scriveners' apprentice boys' and the Committee refused to make a grant to a farmer to enable his daughters to emigrate to the United States.

In 1881 the estates in the Ironmongers' group were formally partitioned between the various Companies involved, though still managed by the Ironmongers. The Scriveners received 1,259 acres, some 4-5 miles south of Coleraine, clustered round the hamlets of Ballywilliam, Killure, Kinnyglass, Drumcroon and Ballylintagh in the parishes of Macosquin and Aghadowey.

In the 1890s the tenants purchased most of their lands from the Scriveners. The Company received a lump sum of £14,383, and anticipated a further £1,200 for the lands not yet contracted for .[7] The Company was well satisfied for the interest on these sums was sufficient to equal the loss of rents, which in some years amounted to over 40 per cent of the Company's entire income. The remaining lands were sold some years later.

A final hurdle was overcome in 1898. Jealous eyes had been cast upon the purchase money. The lawsuit Attorney-General *vs* The Irish Society and others (including the Scriveners), in the High Court of Justice in Ireland, had commenced in 1892. The plaintiffs (the Attorney General and Rev. John Johnston, a nonconformist Ulster minister) alleged that all the Companies held their Ulster property only as trustees, and were therefore not entitled to the purchase money, which should be used for the benefit of the local population.

Fortunately for the Companies, they won the case.[8] So ended the Company's association with Ireland. The Irish Society, towards which the Scriveners' Company paid almost as much as it did towards the Manor of Lizard, continues to function as a landlord to the present day.

23   Detail from the Scriveners' stained glass window presented to Londonderry in 1911.

Appendix VIII
THE SCRIVENER NOTARY TODAY

Brooke's Notary, 11th edition *(London, Sweet & Maxwell 1992)* lists the many activities to be undertaken by a notary as 'the verification of documents to take effect abroad, preparation and translation of documents for use abroad, translation of documents emanating from overseas, protesting bills of exchange, certifying copies, taking affidavits and ... ship protests', but this list begs as many questions as it answers. Why should a notary be a translator of languages? Why should it fall to a notary to protest dishonoured Bills of Exchange? What is a ship protest? And why, once again, should it involve a notary? And why should it be a notary and not, say, a solicitor, who authenticates legal documents for use abroad?

The 5th edition of Brooke's Notary *(London, Stevens & Sons London 1890)* entitled 'A treatise on The Office and Practice of A Notary of England with a full collection of Precedents' casts some interesting light on these questions, not least the nature and extent of notarial practice at the time, for, in the preface the author has this to say *"in endeavouring to make this publication serviceable to the profession, I have at the same time been anxious to render it useful to Bankers and Merchants; and the chapters relating to Bills of Exchange, Promissory Notes, Ship and other Protests, Charterparties, Bottomry Bonds, Powers of Attorney, Commissions from Foreign Courts of Judicature, Declarations substituted for Affidavits and to various instruments connected with Mercantile and Shipping matters, are written with the intention of being of practical use to them"*. Clearly the notary at that time was very much concerned with mercantile law, of which shipping law formed a large part; and the reason for this lay not only, one suspects, in the notary's earlier role as a scrivener, or banker, but also in the nature of the office of a notary where it is stated *"the general functions of a Notary consist in receiving all acts and contracts which require to be clothed with an authentic form ... in establishing their date ... in preserving minutes or originals of acts, and in giving authentic copies of the same (op.cit. p 14).* This, as a general definition, holds true today.

However, domestically, English law has never had much call for the services of a notary. The office is concerned with matters of record in international trade, the notary *clothing in authentic form* mercantile documents for use overseas, and it might be added, preparing such documents. Some of those precedents make interesting reading. The section on shipping, for instance, covers pages 197-276 a third of the total. Here may be found such curiosities as a charterparty for the transportation of coolies from China to Havana (with a gratuity of 600 dollars to the captain *if all his emigrants arrive in good condition,* and a reduction if they did not) *(op.cit p 253)* and precedents for ship protests in consequence of a loss from a gale, or total wreck, or collision at sea. Here, the Master, on arrival, would immediately repair to the office of a Notary to enter a public instrument of protest. Brooke must either have had an intimate knowledge of ships and their ways or a vivid imagination, for here is an extract from one such precedent *(op.cit. p 205) "the gale increased from the South West with a tremendous sea (barometer falling to 26.86). At four a.m. the topmast staysail was blown away and at half past four the ship was pooped by an enormous sea, which smashed into the after cabin, dead lights and doors, flooded the saloon and adjacent cabins, washing all the passengers' luggage etc. about the place ..."* and many pages more in the same vein. However, the notary was not without help if the Master's powers of description, or his own technical knowledge failed him, for there still exist in the offices of a London notary little ship models with moveable yards to assist the Master Mariner in his explanations of how the rig was trimmed as he sat in the notary's office telling his tale. Our merchant fleet has declined, and with it the need for ship's protests, but the shipping business lives on, still part of the work of the office of a Scrivener Notary to this day.[1]

Another curiosity, if one may term it such, concerned the practice of notaries in relation to Bills of Exchange. Once again it was a question of a public act of protest, this time for non-acceptance or non-payment of a Bill or Promissory Note, and it was (and still is) the duty of a notary to make such a protest in respect of foreign bills. The notary had to know his law: in this case, the Bills of Exchange Act 1882, which was reproduced in full in the body of text. The importance of bills and the central role played by notaries may be judged from the fact not only that a substantial part of the book was devoted to the subject, but more intriguingly that in a footnote to the section devoted to Bills of Exchange (p.102) there is a reference to evidence given by *"Messrs Grain, Venn and other notaries [2] before the committee of the House of Commons on Bank Holidays 1867 - 68"*. This business too has declined, but the notary still protests dishonoured foreign Bills.

What about languages? A table at the back of the same edition of Brooke's Notary provided scale fees for translation from Danish or Swedish (two shillings per folio of 72 words) Russian, (seven shillings and sixpence), Latin (two shillings and sixpence) and *all other European languages* (one shilling and ninepence). The linguistic ability was a necessary adjunct of the third major branch of the business of the Notary Public, the certification of Powers of Attorney for use abroad.

Then, as now, Brooke provided information on the formalities required in all the jurisdictions where such powers were to be used, together with precedents for the notarial certificates and precedents for the Powers of Attorney themselves for jurisdictions as diverse as India, the United States, South America, France, Germany, Holland, Switzerland, Spain, Mauritius, Trinidad and Tobago, South Africa, the Notary had to know them all, what form, how many witnesses, what form of proof, what special words, what consular procedures, this knowledge too was part of the stock in trade of the notary. As Brooke says *"the uses and practices of Notaries in England may, in some measure, be considered as traditional … for they are not only transmitted by oral tradition from Notary to apprentice, and from senior Notary to junior Notary, but the Notarial Register Books and the Protest and Noting Books, which are generally preserved with care, and often handed down from one generation of Notaries to another." (preface vii).*

What has changed in the century or so since? In some ways, surprisingly little. Bills of exchange have declined in importance, and with that decline the influence of the profession in the commercial affairs of the City. Ship protests have all but died out, but the shipping practice remains, and so does the translation practice, and so too do the ubiquitous powers of attorney, in ever-increasing numbers. The notary remains outward looking, concerned with affairs of foreign law and procedure. New (or apparently new, for the 1890 edition of Brooke's Notary is silent on the subject) areas of notarial practice have sprung up, such as the giving of expert opinions on foreign law, especially succession law for the Probate Courts, the drawing of wills for British nationals with properties in foreign jurisdictions, advice on property and succession laws of foreign jurisdictions (two notaries are also French *avocats*) and the preparation and attestation of all manner of deeds and documents for use overseas. Scrivener Notaries quietly go about their business, and in so doing make their own unique contribution to oiling the wheels of international commerce. So the Scrivener Notaries' profession, never more than a few score, has successfully reinvented itself to face the needs of a changing world, and can count amongst its number experts in shipping law, in private international law, and in the laws of France and Spain, who lecture, write articles, advise clients on foreign laws and procedures and whose society, the Society of Scrivener Notaries of London, is now a full member of the *Union Internationale du Notariat Latin*. This is proof, if proof were needed, that the London notary, the Scrivener Notary, has never been held in higher esteem. Their full story remains to be told.

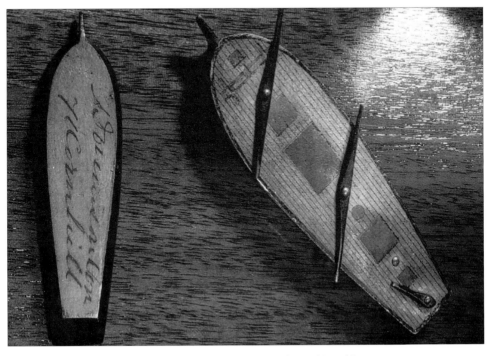

24 Models of ships used by notaries when taking ship protests.

Appendix IX
List of Manuscripts

In the Guildhall Library

MS.366(16) Case of the Company as to the legality of an assessment on its members towards the rebuilding of their Hall burnt in the Great Fire. With opinion of Sir Thomas Raymond, 14 May 1674.

5370 The 'Common Paper'—the subject of Steer's work, pp.xiii, XIV. This includes Assistants' Lists 1554-5, 1562-3, 1569, 1575, 1580-1, 1587, 1601. Membership subscription oaths from 1417.

6199 Extracts from Court minutes (now untraceable), 1696-1820, chiefly relating to the purchase of the Company's Hall by the Coachmakers' Company and to other premises belonging to the Scriveners' Company, compiled c.1830.

8716 Original charter of incorporation granted to the Company by King James I, 28 January 1616/7.

8717 Original ordinances, ratified 29 January 1618/9.

8718 Original ordinances, ratified 28 May 1635.

8719 Copy of grant of arms and supporters, originally granted 11 November 1634, made at the Company's request by Stephen Peters, arms painter, 1738.

8720 Wardens' account book, 1732-1894.

8721 Members' rolls, recording admission to freedom and livery, and offices served, 1732-1892. (There are 84 rolls, but the record is incomplete.)

8721A Photostat copy of MS. Rawlinson D51 in the Bodleian Library, Oxford. This record is included in Steer's work pp.xvi-xviii.

8722 Bond in £1,000 by the Coachmakers' Company to the Scriveners' Company, 13 May 1703.

8723 Copy bargain and sale by Sir Arthur Savage and Dame Sarah his wife (late wife of George Smithies, Alderman of London, dec'd) and others, to Charles Bostock, Citizen and Scrivener, of a great messuage with garden known as Bacon House in Oat Lane, St Mary Staining, City of London 10 June 1628; with copy fine appertaining, 8 July 1628.

9837 Deed of arrangement between (a) the Brewers' Company, the Scriveners' Company, the Corporation of London, the Pewterers' Company, the Barbersurgeons' Company and the Carpenters' Company, and (b) the Ironmongers' Company, in relation to matters arising out of the Londonderry Estates, 20 November 1884.

In the Bodleian Library, Oxford, Relating to The Scriveners' Company

Rawlinson MS.D51 (S.C.12869), being records of the Company of Scriveners transcribed in the time of Charles II (see Steer, *Common Paper*, p.xvii).

Rawlinson MS.D734 (S.C.13504). Miscellaneous papers relating to the City of London and including:

i   Petition to King Charles II on the issue of a Quo Warranto against the Company, expressing their submission, but praying for continuance of such privileges as he shall think fit (f.79).

ii Two copies of a petition to the Lord Mayor and Aldermen respecting the binding of apprentices, with statement of reasons, and letter, 1672 (ff.80-87).

iii Counsel's opinion, by Sir Thomas Raymond, 14 May 1674, in favour of the power of the Company to levy contributions upon the members for the rebuilding of the Hall, burned down in the Fire of London (f.88).

Rawlinson MS.D911 (S.C.13677). Fragmentary English papers, historical and legal, but including (f.196), 'The explanac'on of the clause concerninge scriveners, etc. conteyned in the Act against usury made in the xxi yeare of Kinge James'.

Notes

Chapter 1

1. J.R. Green, *A Short History of the English People* (1889) pp 93 and 196-199.
2. 22 Henry VII (1530/31) Chapter 4.
3. M. Birks, *Gentlemen of the Law* (1960)
4. Nigel Ramsay, 'Forgery and the Rise of the London Scriveners Company' in *Fakes and Frauds* (1988), pp 99-108.
5. Mayor's Remembrancer Rolls at Guildhall.
6. *Common Paper*, p 66.
7. See *Writings to the Court* (1987) which illustrates the Lord Mayor's command.
8. The Troubles of a Scrivener from the *Regiment of Princes*, published in *Writings to the Court* (1987).
9. W.W. Skeat (ed.), *The Complete Works of Geoffrey Chaucer* (1923), p.236. Extract in Francis W. Steer, *A History of the Worshipful Company of Scriveners*, Vol.I, p.67.

Chapter 2

1. There were two parliaments held in 1388. At the second, held in Cambridge, there were enactments regulating beggars and common nuisances, as well as labourers. Craftsmen, including writers and copyists, were usually found as street traders, their stalls being their shops.
2. The will of William Smith, Citizen and Joyner of London, son and heir of William Smith, Citizen and Joyner of London deceased, who was the son and heir of Richard Smith, Citizen and Coffermaker of London, also deceased, direct ancestors of the co-author, is dated 13 July *1638 (Archdeaconry of London*, proved 29 September 1638). It cites the deed of sale of property in St. Anne's Lane, St. John Zachary to Richard Smith by the two scriveners, John Lulton and Bartholomew Brookesby, 22 May 3 Edward VI (1549).
3. This cheque fetched £260 at the first old cheque auction held at Stanley Gibbons in February 1981.
4. *Dictionary of National Biography* and Uvedale Lambert, *History of Bletchingley* (1921) pp.278-280 and 351-2.
5. See page 48.

Chapter 3

1. Dr Steer wrote a chapter on the Company's Hall in his *History*, but since then further information about the Hall has come to light. This chapter is derived from a talk given to the Scriveners' Company by Stephen Freeth, City Archivist and Honorary Liveryman of the Scriveners' Company, on 13 July 1993. See also Guildhall MSS 28, 935 and 28, 941-3.
2. Francis W. Steer, *History*, Vol.I, p.23.

Chapter 4

1. *The London Tradesman* (1747), p.322.
2. Chancery Proceedings (PRO C 11/2872/20).
3. Chancery Proceedings (PRO C 11/991/10).
4. Chancery Proceedings (PRO C 11/2250/56).
5. Chancery Proceedings 28 January 1723 (PRO C 11/1819/3). This man is likely to have been Sir John Thornicroft who was called to the bar in 1686 and created a baronet in 1701. *Alumni Cantabrigienses*, vol.IV (Cambridge, 1927), p.232. See also *Complete Baronetage*, Vol.V (1906), p.71.
6. They have been published by the London Record Society under the title *London Politics 1713-1717. Minutes of a Whig Club 1714-1717*, edited by H. Horwitz (London, 1981).
7. They were published by the London Record Society in the volume edited by W.A. Speck and W.A. Gray which is mentioned above.

8.   Romney Sedgwick, *The House of Commons 1715-1754*, vol.II (London: 1970), pp.177-8.
9.   *Dictionary of English Furniture Makers 1660-1840*, edited by Geoffrey Beard and Christopher Gilbert (Leeds, 1986).
10. PRO B 1/23.
11. A notice of his death in *Musgrave's Obituary* describes him as 'of Threadneedle Street, Scrivener'. He was buried on 8 October 1728 at the Church of St Benet Fink.
12. Corporation of London Records Office-C. Companies 710.
13. P.R.O., PRO B 11/803.

Chapter 5

1.   Attorneys were originally admitted to practise in the Courts of King's Bench and Common Pleas. Solicitors were admitted to the Court of Chancery. These distinctions became blurred in the 18th century and had virtually disappeared by the 19th century. Robert Robson, *The Attorney in Eighteenth Century England* (Cambridge, 1959) pp.149, 151-2.
2.   The Company's accounts for 21 October 1749 contain an entry reading 'Pd Mr John Hodges in full for his bill for printing 500 copies of the case of the Free Scriveners of London'.
3.   Scriveners' Company Accounts 29 May 1752.
4.   *The Records of the Society of Gentlemen Practisers in the Courts of Law and Equity and called the Law Society.* Introduction by Edwin Freshfield (London, 1897). Freshfield was himself a Scrivener and Master of the Company in 1885, and also the donor of two silver-gilt cups.
5.   A. Glover (ed.), *The Life of Samuel Johnson, L.L.D.* by James Boswell, Esq: vol.2 (1926), p.237.

Chapter 6

1.   Freedom Records of the City of London—February 1763.
2.   Law lists 1793 and 1810.
3.   The faculties of notaries public are at Lambeth Palace Library. They usually give the diocese in which the notary was born or, in the case of notaries from abroad, the exact birthplace.
4.   P.R.O. PRO B 11/1177.
5.   Wright, C., and Foyle, G.E., *History of Lloyd's* (London, 1928), pp.387-9.
6.   P.R.O., PROB 11/1339.
7.   Samuel, E R., 'Anglo-Jewish Notaries and Scriveners' (paper read before The Jewish Historical Society of England, 20 December 1949).
8.   Robert Shank's precedent book is in Brian Brooks's possession.
9.   Records in the possession of the Society of Scrivener Notaries, London.
10. John Forster, *The Life of Charles Dickens* (London, 1893), p.18.
11. *Scots Magazine*, vol.53, p.623.

Chapter 7

1.   *Gentleman's Magazine.*
2.   Joseph Foster, *Admissions to the Middle Temple.*
3.   P.R.O., PROB 11/1467.
4.   P.R.O., PROB 11/1355.
5.   Registers of annual practising certificates for notaries - Lambeth Palace Library F III/6/2.
6.   *Post Office London Directory*, 1846.
7.   *Post Office London Directory*, 1827.
8.   Parish Registers of Framfield, deposited at East Sussex Record Office, Lewes.
9.   Information given to Brian Brooks by the late Philip H. Blake, F.H.G.
10. *Kent's London Directories* 1774 and 1780.
11. *Holden's Triennial Directory*, 1805-6-7.
12. St Mary Woolnoth burial registers, Guildhall Library Ms 7639A.
13. *Law Lists.*
14. At St George's Church.
15. *Law List 1825.*
16. Information about Christopher Sundius's background and life in Sweden was supplied to Brian Brooks in 1952 by the Universitetsbiblioket, Lund and the Riksarkivet in Stockholm.
17. *Holden's Triennial Directory* 1805-6-7.
18. Information about Sundius's Nonconformist connections was supplied to Brian Brooks in 1952 by the London Missionary Society.
19. P.R.O., PROB 11/1848.

20. *Dictionary of National Biography.*
21. P.R.O., PROB 11/ 1988.
22. *Dictionary of National Biography.*
23. *Dictionary of National Biography.*
24. *Kelly's Handbook to the Titled, Landed and Official Classes.*

Chapter 8

1. He became a freeman of the Company on 25 July 1883 and served as Master 1899-1900. His wife and the wife of the second John Venn were sisters.
2. Minutes of the Court Meeting of 29 July 1914.
3. The Company's Barge Standard is displayed in Stationers' Hall.
4. See *Complete Baronetage*, Vol.V (1906), p.71.

Appendix I

1. He was a Warden of the Scriveners' Company—see Appendix III.

Appendix II

1. Extracted from *Poems upon Divers Occasions with Character of a London Scrivener* printed for John Crosley, bookseller in Oxford, 1667. This work has been attributed to Jeremias Wells (1646-1679) who in 1667 was a 21-year-old student at St John's College, Oxford, and who subsequently became curate of All Hallows, Barking. *Alumni Oxonienses* 1500-1714, J. Foster.

Appendix IV

1. Sir Ernest Pooley, *The Guilds of the City of London* (William Collins, London, 1945), p.40.
2. Francis W.Steer, ed., *Scriveners' Common Paper 1357-1628, With a Continuation to 1678*, London Record Society, 1968, p.58.
3. Steer, *op. cit.*, p.40.
4. Steer, *op. cit.*, p.59 (see also p.116).
5. Corporation of London Record Office, 'Index of Scriveners', bond No.40.
6. Steer, *op. cit.*, p.123. See also Francis W. Steer, *A history of the Worshipful Company of Scriveners of London* (Phillimore, London and Chichester, 1973), pp.46-8.
7. C.L.R.O. CFI/2?; 5; 21?; 25?; 37; 57?; 116?; 134?; 137?; 215; 235; 301 (these are bundles of certificates of freedom by month and those marked ? include more than one signed by Braxton).
8. C.L.R.O. CFI/137. See also C.R.J. Humphery-Smith, *Writings to the Court: a Scrivener's Miscellany*, 1987, p.15.
9. C.L.R.O., CFI/767.
10. C.L.R.O., CFI/116.
11. C.L.R.O., CFI/215.
12. C.L.R.O., CFI/301.
13. C.L.R.O., CFI/25.
14. C.L.R.O., CFI/137. For Barton and Browne see also Humphery-Smith, *op. cit.*, p.15.
15. C.L.R.O., CFI/559.
16. C.L.R.O., CFI/603.
17. C.L.R.O., CFI/686. William Brady was Master of the Company in April 1756 (CFI/813), freedom by redemption of Thomas Bullock.
18. C.L.R.O., CFI/719.
19. C.L.R.O., CFI/780.
20. C.L.R.O., CFI/1158.
21. C.L.R.O., CFI/1194.
22. C.L.R.O., CFI/1220 (Shaw); 1289 (Scougall).
23. C.L.R.O., CFI/1317.

Appendix V: Scrivener Freemen

1. Original Wills from the Prerogative Court of Canterbury are referred to by clerks' quires. The Public Record Office call numbers for the corresponding microfilm copies are also cited.
2. 's' means servitude. Servitude was usually by indentured agreement with a master. 'p' means patrimony, by virtue of a father or grandfather's livery before birth. 'r' means redemption by proposal and payment of a fine. 'n.g.' means not given, but estimated.

Appendix V: Scrivener Aldermen

1. A.B. Beaven, *The Aldermen of the City of London* (1908 and 1913).
2. The original edition of *D.N.B.* makes his Alderman's Service continuous from 1670 to 1688, ignoring his ejection in 1683 and also his 18 years' tenure of office after his restoration.
3. *D.N.B.* ignores his connection with St Bartholomew's Hospital and with the Honourable Artillery Company, although the former was continuous for 25 years, and the latter for 33 years.

Appendix VII

1. This contribution is taken from a talk given to the Scriveners' Company by Stephen Freeth on 12 July 1994.
2. *Londonderry and the London Companies, 1609-1629* (HMSO, 1928).
3. Guildhall MS 28941.
4. *G.E.C.Complete Baronetage, Clark's Heraldry* (1974), p.231.
5. Steer, *History*, Vol.I, p.1.
6. MS 28937.
7. MS 28932.
8. MS 28941.

Appendix VIII

1. The ship-owners were grateful for these services. Framed photographs of the Finnish four masted barque Herzogin Cecile *becalmed in the South Atlantic,* (the Australian grain trade), the Penang, the German barque Priwall in Iquique 1927 (the guano trade) the Olivebank, Andrew Weir & Co, (an unlucky line, apparently) the Swedish four masted barque C.B. Pederson, *Sydney to the channel for orders on the line* and other representatives of the age of sale dating from the 1920s adorn the walls of the author's office.
2. The Grain and the Venn families provided many generations of notaries, the last members retiring well within living memory.

Select Bibliography

Scriveners' Company Common Paper 1357-1628 with a continuation to 1678, Edited by Francis W. Steer, London Record Society, 1968 with some additions.

Abbott, J.A.R., 'Robert Abbott, City Money Scrivener, and his account book 1646-1652', *Guildhall Miscellany*, no.7 (August 1956), pp.30-39.

Aldous, V.E., *My Ancestors were Freemen of the City of London* (London, 1999).

Beaven A.B., *The Aldermen of the City of London* (1908, 1913).

Birks, M., *Gentlemen of the Law* (1960).

Bromley, J. and Child, H., *The Armorial Bearings of the Guilds of London* (1960).

Brooke, C.N.L., '*Approaches to Medieval Forgery*', J. Soc. Archivists iii (1965-9), pp.577-86.

Brooks, C.W., Hemholz, R.M., Stein, P.G., *Notaries Public in England since the Reformation* (Norwich, 1991).

Cheney, C.R., *Notaries Public in England in the Thirteenth and Fourteenth Centuries* (1972).

City of London Livery Companies' Commission.

Coleman, D.C., 'London Scriveners and the Estate Market in the Later Seventeenth Century', *Economic History Review*, Second series, vol.IV, no.2 (1951), pp.221-30.

Coulton, G.G., *Social Life in Britain from the Conquest to the Reformation* (1919).

Ditchfield, P.H., *The City Companies of London and their good works* (1904), pp.310-13.

Freshfield, E., 'Some Notarial Marks in the "Common Paper" of the Scriveners' Company', *Archaeologia*, vol.54 (1895), pp.239-54.

Freshfield, E., *The Records of the Society of Gentlemen Practisers* (London, 1897).

Gutteridge, H.C., 'The Origin and Historical Development of the Profession of Notaries Public in England', *Cambridge Legal Essays written in honour of and presented to Doctor Bond, Professor Buckland and Professor Kenny* (1926), pp.123-37.

Hector, L.C., *Palaeography and Forgery*, St Anthony's Hall Publication No.15 (1959).

Jackson, Donald, *The Story of Writing* (1981).

Jenkinson, H., *The Later Court Hands in England, from the Fifteenth to the Seventeenth Century* (1927).

Phillips, T., *Londonderry and the London Companies, 1609-1629, being a survey and other documents submitted to King Charles I* (1928).

Purvis, J.S., *Notarial Signs from the York Archiepiscopal Records* (1957).

Purvis, J.S., 'The Notary Public in England', *Archivum,* vol.12 (1926), pp.121-6.

Ramsay, Nigel, 'Forgery and the rise of the London Scriveners' Company', *Fakes and Frauds* (1988), pp.99-108.

Rawlinson, M.S., D51, in the Bodleian Library, Oxford.

Ready, N.P., *Brooke's Notary* (10th edition) (London, 1988).

Reddaway, T., 'The Livery Companies of Tudor London', *History*, vol.51 (1966), pp.287-99.

Richardson, H.G., 'The Forgery of Fines, 1272-1376', *English Historical Review* XXXV (1920), pp.405-18.

Riley, H.T. (ed.), *Memorials of London and London life, in the XIIIth, XIVth, and XVth centuries* (1868).

Sharpe, R.R. (ed.), *Calendar of Letter-Books [A-L] preserved among the Archives of the Corporation of the City of London at the Guildhall*, 11vols. (1899-1912).

Thornley, J.C. and Hastings, G.W. (eds.), *The Guilds of the City of London and their Liverymen* (n.d.), pp.220-2.

Unwin, G., *The Gilds and Companies of London* (4th ed.), 1963.

Venn, J., *Annals of a Clerical Family* (London, 1904)

Warrell, W., *Scribes ancient and modern (Otherwise Law Writers or Scriveners)*, 1889.

Nearly all the titles mentioned above give references to other sources; see also W.F. Kahl, *The Development of London Livery Companies: an historical essay and a select bibliography* (Boston, Mass., 1960). There are numerous incidental references to the Worshipful Company of Scriveners in general works on the Guilds and in several of the histories of other Livery Companies.

Index